W9-CPP-502
HURON COUNTY LIBRARY
2 008 236742 4

CASTLE OF QUEBEC

JOAN ELSON MORGAN

1949

J. M. DENT & SONS (CANADA) LIMITED

TORONTO : VANCOUVER

Copyright, 1949
by
Joan Elson Morgan

Published by
J. M. DENT & SONS (CANADA) LIMITED

First Printing,
June, 1949

No part of this book may be reproduced in any form without permission in writing from the publisher, except by a reviewer who wishes to quote brief passages in connection with a review written for inclusion in magazine, newspaper or radio broadcast.

PRINTED AND BOUND IN CANADA
T. H. Best Printing Co., Limited, Toronto
This book is set in 11 on 13 point Times Roman type.

FOREWORD

TO TELL THE STORY of the château on the heights of Quebec is to unfold the history of the city itself. This book, *Castle of Quebec,* could well be termed a brief history of the City of Quebec, with particular attention focussed on the castles that have successively occupied the historic site on the cliffs.

Until the early part of the nineteenth century, the people who settled and built Quebec moved within the walls or within the shadow of a great grey building known as the Château St. Louis. In 1834 a spectacular fire burned down this old Château which had been completed in its earliest form in 1647 by Governor Montmagny, successor to Samuel Champlain who had founded the city in 1608. Before the end of the nineteenth century, a baronial structure in Norman design filled the void left by the destruction of the Château St. Louis, and from the day of the official opening of the Château Frontenac in December, 1893, all the world has had access to this fine hostelry.

It would seem that destiny chose well the scenes of her history-making dramas when she selected Quebec and the châteaux on the cliff for the successive events that have commemorated that site from 1620 to the present time.

The story of the men and women whose paths crossed the threshold of the two châteaux of Quebec will be told within the limits of this book, the aim of which is, first, to afford a source of true information regarding these interesting people (with due regard to that which is admittedly legendary), and secondly, to present the facts in such a straightforward narrative form that the reader need not be weightily conscious of reading just another history. Some of these facts are well known; some are little known; others are known only to those few who painstakingly unearth them from the archives and the unsuspected places. It is admitted that historians do not all agree on every point; in such cases the author has followed only the most reliable sources. (A bibliography appears in the final pages of this book.)

For the countless thousands of people who come to Quebec yearly, there is scarcely the opportunity nor the time for them to delve into the many sources of information which the author has consulted in two years of intensive study. Quebec is rich in material which the average vacationing visitor cannot reasonably hope to investigate no matter how keen his interest. Another object of this book, then, is to give the tourist as well as the student the benefit of the writer's research in connection with the historic events that have made Quebec what it is today. The treasures of literature and art that lie in the Provincial and Federal archives, museums and libraries have been consulted; newspapers, preserved since 1764, have been perused at length, as well as correspondence covering the French and English régimes; and considerable advantage has been taken of the kind permission granted by the Canadian Pacific Railway Company to study the oldest files in its archives. Furthermore, the author has resided in Quebec for three years for the purpose of becoming familiar with the landmarks of history and to acquire the touch of authenticity so necessary for a work of this nature.

The author is convinced that such a rich and colourful story is well worth telling, that it is in itself its own justification. If the criticism be made that too little space has been given to certain events as important as those dealt with at length in this work, it is refuted by the fact that this is the story of a building, that the building has been kept predominant as far as possible, in the belief that the reader, in search of information on the châteaux of Quebec, would prefer it so.

The romance of a proud building and its historical predecessor is the theme of *Castle of Quebec*.

J. E. M.

PROLOGUE

Quebec, thy name with magic power can start
The peace-bound pulses of the warrior's heart;
Above thy rocks a burning halo plays
To light the record of departed days . . .
(From W. F. Hawley's poem *Quebec*. 1829)[1]

Past and present are one in Quebec; the spirit of "departed days" is a part of today. The streets of the city are those of yesteryear; the ancient names are still heard; the faith and many of the customs are the same; the language of the people is that of the first white people who settled Quebec nearly three and a half centuries ago—those intrepid French pioneers whose descendants still inhabit the city. The buildings of the colonizers still stand, with few exceptions. . . . In Quebec, Time has been kind and destroyed very little.

"Je me souviens". Quebec remembers her heritage. Long ago an imposing French château stood on the heights of Quebec. It was destroyed by fire in 1834. The few remaining stones of that stronghold—the Fort and Château St. Louis—are unavoidably hidden in the walls and beneath the foundation of the lovely castle which has replaced it, the Château Frontenac. A vast monument to the dramatic history that brought Quebec into being, it is fitting that the Château Frontenac should be a replica of a château of old Normandy, symbolic of the old France of Quebec's Founder, Samuel de Champlain, and that the men who built it should have named it after the gallant French count who strove to make its forerunner the most elegant château that early Canada's conditions and France's treasury would permit, and chose as its crest the Comte de Frontenac's Coat of Arms.

Castle of Quebec tells of these two famous châteaux, what happened to make them so, to make Quebec the enchanted place it is today.

[1]From a privately printed book called *Quebec, the Harp and Other Poems*, by W. F. Hawley. No trace of copyright can be found, and all efforts to trace any descendants of the Hawley family have been fruitless. The volume consulted by the author was found in the library of the Literary and Historical Society in Quebec City.

To My Sister
MADGE,
with love
and admiration

Chapter One

High on the Cape he stood, and cast his eye
O'er the deep forest and unclouded sky—
Proudly beneath him roll'd a sunlit tide . . .

W. F. HAWLEY.

IT IS THE SUMMER of 1620 and Samuel de Champlain is once again landing at Quebec, returning from one of his many visits to his homeland. This time there stands at his side a lovely lady of delicate stature and graceful air, wearing a simple gown of excellent quality; she is Marie-Hélène Boullé, Madame de Champlain. They had been married in December, 1610,[1] while Champlain was on a previous visit to France. Then she was but a child of twelve; now she is a beautiful young woman.

Champlain is a noble figure, dominating his wife's small stature. His hair is long, dark and curling; he wears a moustache and an imperial, which are the fashion of his day. The full sleeves of his coat are slashed; about his neck is a broad linen collar fastened in front with cord and tassels.[2] He carries a broad-brimmed hat with a dark plume.

Quebec is not wearing its best on this particular day, even though it is mid-summer, but Marie-Hélène is overjoyed to be safely on land again after the long uncertain voyage. Yet she is scarcely happy at the sight of the tiny cluster of buildings hemmed in by a rain-misted river and dense forests, and overhung by a darkly forbidding cliff.

[1]In *The Works of Samuel de Champlain,* a translation of Champlain's Journals by six Canadian scholars, edited by H. P. Biggar, and published by The Champlain Society, Toronto, 1925, we find that the marriage settlement was "done and executed at Paris in the house of the said Boullé and his wife, situated in Paris in the said street and parish of St. Germain . . . . after noon in the year 1610, Monday the twenty-seventh day of December;" and that special mention was made to the effect that "nevertheless it has been agreed, in consideration of the tender age of the said Hélène Boullé shall not be carried out and effected until two years elapsed and completed from this day . . ."

[2]This description is taken from *Champlain's Voyages,* a publication of The Prince Society, Boston, 1881.

A carefully nurtured girl, daughter of one of the King's secretaries, Marie-Hélène Boullé had spent her life amidst elegance and plenty. How was she to endure what now faced her?

Two months at sea on a vaguely charted course, in a small and ill-equipped ship which had been tossed hither and yon in the most alarming manner, had afflicted Marie-Hélène — as it would most people — with an overwhelming seasickness. She was weak and weary as she disembarked on the soil of New France with her middle-aged husband to be presented with all the flourish of old France to the few tattered citizens of Quebec who had gathered at the river's edge. The heart of the intrepid explorer must have been heavy as he led her across the threshold of the deplorably neglected habitation that was to be her home in the New World until he had accomplished the considerable task of building a more suitable home for her.

Several relatives of Champlain accompanied them on this occasion, so we are told, but history does not oblige us with their names. Three waiting maids accompanied Madame de Champlain. They were her only companions.[3]

Obviously the habitation had been built too quickly in that significant year, 1608, and now, twelve years later, after the Founder's recent two-year absence, it was but a ramshackle pile scarcely bearing resemblance to a dwelling. The men whom he had left in charge of it had certainly failed him, probably having been too busy in their fight for existence — how could they be sure that Champlain would ever return?—consequently one wing of the building had collapsed completely, and the storeroom gave indication that it would do the same with the help of the next high wind. The rain trickled dismally through the leaky roof of the section that was to be their dwelling; drafts and daylight filtered through the crevices in the walls.

Little wonder that dainty Marie-Hélène, scarcely out of her teens,[4] was quite overcome by the prospect and retired, at the earliest opportunity, to the small bare room set apart for her

[3]J. M. Le Moine, *Quebec, Past and Present,* (1894).

[4]Dr. William Kingsford in *History of Canada,* Vol. I. (Roswell & Hutchison, Toronto, (1887) says that Madame de Champlain was twenty. All historians are not agreed on this point.

personal use, to place there a crucifix and to kneel before it, shivering and despairing, seeking courage from the faith she had so recently adopted to please her husband.

At the junction of the St. Lawrence and St. Charles rivers which bound two sides of Quebec City, there is an historic point of land. The lower section of the city now sprawls upon it. The streets of St. Peter and St. Paul cut across it. Once it was the site of the rough habitation that was Champlain's home and headquarters before his Fort St. Louis was built. Today, the little Church of Notre Dame des Victoires stands near the place where the habitation once stood.

As the habitation was rather typical of Canada's housing in the earliest days, a description of it is interesting. It consisted of several buildings of which three, somewhat larger than the others, were joined together. In size, each was about eighteen feet by fifteen feet. All three were set in a small courtyard wherein also stood a watch-tower that overlooked the buildings and the river. At the second-story level, a gallery encircled the three buildings. Five cannon, and a ditch sixteen feet wide by six feet deep, with a drawbridge, protected the three sides facing the river. All was enclosed by a stout wooden palisade. The structures were made of roughly hewn logs and planks which, having been placed hastily together, were constantly in need of attention.

Far from discouraged by the plight in which he found everything, Champlain thanked God that the settlement and his men were still in existence. He set about the reparation of the buildings and the preparation of stronger defences against the Indians. It was a major problem not only to get materials but to get labourers. Louis Hébert had come out to Quebec with his wife in 1617, and was trying to build a home halfway up the cliff in a spot that was still deeply forested and quite unprotected. Hébert had prevailed upon Champlain's men to assist him.[5] Then, too, a small group of Recollet priests had come out and were labouring to build a monastery and a chapel on the banks of the St. Charles River. The men who were not helping Hébert gladly lent a hand to the Fathers. Since there were only fifty men in the whole colony, one wonders how Champlain managed.

[5]J. M. Le Moine, *Quebec, Past and Present.*

The first really happy event that occurred after Madame de Champlain landed was a visit from her brother, Eustache, who had come to New France some time previously. Since neither, it seems, knew of the other's presence in the New World, their meeting was a particularly joyous reunion. Champlain was delighted to have this unexpected guest, not only for the valuable assistance Eustache would (and did) give him, but more especially for the cheering effect his presence had upon Marie-Hélène. It is easy to imagine them on that first evening together, exchanging the scanty news from home, discussing the fine strong fort that Champlain would soon begin building and which was to be a worthy home for the First Lady of New France.

Gradually Marie-Hélène's courage was renewed. She began to go about the settlement, bringing faith and help to those less fortunate than herself. She made friends easily with the children of the few amiable Indians who, in fear of the hostile and more powerful tribes, had attached themselves to the little French colony.

Like the thousands who were destined to come after her to this matchless corner of Canada, Marie-Hélène de Champlain fell under the spell of its beauty. What did she see on a summer day, as she stood on the crest of the cliff near the place where her husband's men toiled to erect a stronghold? A panorama of land and water such as is not often unrolled in a single picture. Rich green forests covering the deeply curving hills stretched to the warm blue horizon; between the hills sparkled a magnificent river, blinding the eyes with the sun upon it, and reflecting the passing of a stray cloud blown by the summer breeze . . . Surely the land was more verdant here than in all Europe! Was it possible that the sky was more blue? . . . Was that river purer and brighter than the rivers of France, or did it only seem so? . . . In sombre contrast to the ocean of colour that rose all round her, there were the grey and venerable rocky cliffs on the opposite shore from Quebec which were almost a match in height and ruggedness for those they faced and upon which she stood. White winged gulls glided leisurely through the quiet air to rest at last on the surface of the river. And then Marie-Hélène's eyes would follow the river to its curve westward. There lay the unexplored and unknown country so intriguing to her husband and so frightening to her.

The Champlains were proud folk. So skilfully did they cloak their miseries that none were able to discern or record them. They endured in dignified silence the innumerable privations and hardships that were the lot of all who believed in the New World and dared to challenge its primitive supremacy. Only when his colony and his fort were at stake did Champlain humble himself to plead again and again for help from the Company in France which held the commission for colonization in New France. Previously, during the years between 1610 and 1618, he had made several trips to France to place the desperate needs of the colony before the King and the Company but had obtained only promises which, though possibly sincere at the time, did not materialize to any extent. And so the months passed in which Champlain continued to fight savages in the New World and clever courtesans in the Old, gaining very slight advantage over either.

It was not until 1621 that King Louis XIII (after whom Champlain's fort was eventually named) sent him, in accordance with a promise made two years earlier, a supply of arms and ammunition that was ridiculously inadequate considering the swarms of hostile Iroquois in the surrounding forests. There was little the harassed colonizer could do but build the fort as quickly as the few hands could accomplish it, of a size to hold all the colonists in time of attack, and garrison it with as many men as he could muster.

Meanwhile, the fragile beauty and gentleness of Madame de Champlain were winning the hearts of the entire settlement. If she had great longing still for the comfortable world she had left behind her, it was kept carefully locked in her heart, and she talked only of "the home on the mountain" of which she would some day be mistress. But the intermittent and nerve-wracking attacks of the various Indian tribes were a test of her courage such as she had never imagined possible. Fortunately, no concerted attack was made by the savages in those early years. Possibly they, like France itself, doubted the importance or the permanence of the wretched little group who, straggling up the side of a rocky cliff, proposed to strike root and found a new world.

Those early winters in Quebec were miserably destitute of

creature comforts as we know them today. In the summer, as much time as possible was spared from work on the fort to plant and tend gardens. Nevertheless, the produce grown was far from sufficient to afford three meals a day for each person until spring should bring ships from home. They grew peas, beans, corn, cabbage and wheat, and hopefully planted grape vines. They gathered all the wild produce that grew within safe distance around the settlement. Yet winter always found them with pitifully little in their makeshift cellars. They hunted whenever ammunition could be spared, but the skill of trapping had yet to be learned from the Indians. They caught fish and smoked them, and ate quantities of smoked eels which made them ill. When the ships from France, bearing precious supplies, were late or did not come at all, the people were reduced to eating roots. Most of them suffered from scurvy and many died from it.

According to Champlain's own record, Quebec, in 1622, had a population of fifty, which included men, women and children, and in the two succeeding years there was an increase of eleven. By 1623, after three years' labour, Champlain had little more than a shallow hole in the rock of the cliff and was still without sufficient material with which to build the fort.

It was at this time the Father of New France realized that in order to facilitate work on the fort, they must somehow cut a road up the mountain from the shore to the spot where the fort was being constructed. Since the lower slopes of the mountain were heavily forested, the road was little more than a cleared passage through the trees. But they were all very proud of it, these trail blazers of the past, and they called it Mountain Way. More than three hundred years later, when it had become a street, it was named Mountain Hill and now connects the Upper and Lower sections of the City.

With much toil the road was ready for use on November 29th, 1623, and from then on the fort showed greater progress. The walls began to rise out of the wilderness and there was hope in the hearts of the destitute few who looked to it as their salvation.

The courage of the great Colonizer could never for a moment have been questioned during all his trials. But the courage of his fragile wife was dependent upon her state of health which was becoming increasingly delicate. In spite of the fact that her husband has left us no mention of her in his journals, we cannot doubt that Marie-Hélène made an heroic attempt to withstand the rigours of the climate, the scarcity of food, the deprivation of personal necessities, the constant, nerve-paralyzing threat of a horrible death at the hands of the Indians.

Though she had been born a Huguenot, Champlain had brought about the conversion of Marie-Hélène to the Catholic faith, and so fervent had she become that she now expressed a wish to retire to a cloister. This must have been a great blow to her husband. While he lived he refused her his permission to do so.

There came a day of heart-breaking calamity for the colony of Quebec. On April 20th, 1624,[6] the wind blew too strongly round the high bluffs and whisked off part of the new roof of the fort and deposited it below the brow of the cliff.

Then it was that Champlain knew Marie-Hélène could stay no longer in New France. To save her life he must take her home again. Four months later, on August 15th, 1624, they sailed for France and remained there together the following year.

Upon his departure for France with his wife in 1624, Champlain left instructions with his men that the work on the fort must be pushed with all possible speed in his absence. Nevertheless, when he returned in 1626, he was met with conditions not dissimilar to those which had greeted him in 1620 when he had found his habitation in ruins. This time, however, he was not accompanied by his wife. She had remained in France with her parents.

The habitation, still in use, was once more in a deplorable state, and the fort (now named St. Louis after the young King Louis XIII) showed negligible progress. Champlain again applied his courage and initiative to the job at hand. Always convinced that defence was of paramount importance, he proceeded to mount four cannon on the bluff side of the fort to cover attack from the river. On the other sides, facing the dense forest then covering the slopes, he erected a stout wooden palisade, stronger even than that which encircled the habitation. He still hoped that the King would send him soldiers to garrison it.

[6]L'Abbé C. H. Laverdière's *Oeuvres de Champlain,* (1870).

The following winter the weather was the greatest obstacle. It was a long winter, intensely cold, and there seemed no end to the snow. All through the season it lay four to five feet deep everywhere. The settlers had no sleighs or sleds; they had neither horses nor oxen to draw them. They knew nothing of the excellent methods of winter transport that were later invented, which have turned Canadian winter into the most exciting and exhilarating season of the whole year.

Scarcely had the fort attained a measure of completion so that it could be used, if necessary, for a defensive shelter, than the Iroquois Five Nations went on the warpath. Possibly these wily redmen foresaw a threat to their domain in the poor huddle of buildings that was Quebec in 1627. By this time they had become aware that these palefaces were not of supernatural origin, as they had at first believed them to be, but were merely beings possessed of much the same unspiritual propensities as themselves.

The tribes of Hurons, Algonquins and Montagnais were of a more peaceable nature, had eagerly exchanged their furs for such articles as the French could or would part with, and it was among these tribes that some small success in Christianizing was achieved. The Iroquois remained aloof and antagonistic, not only to the French but to those less powerful tribes of Indians who trafficked with the newcomers.

Because of his weakness and vulnerability, Champlain was inevitably compelled to ally his little band with the amiable tribes who were enemies of the flint-hearted Iroquois. The next fifty years were to prove most cruelly what dangerous strategy this was — and yet — if it had not been adopted, Quebec might have been wiped out in the space of a few weeks.

The settlers were kept in a state of constant terror, ever on the alert for their lives. Many times a day everyone had to retire to the enclosure of the fort (still not ready for habitation) as war screams echoed in the surrounding woods. The horrors of those days when no one was safe except within the palisade—and only then if well armed—have been well recorded.

War broke out between England and France in July, 1627. As a direct result of it, the longed for and desperately needed supplies from France could not get through to Quebec, thereby adding the peril of starvation to those that already beset the little colony. Disease was rampant in the colony that winter and several of the brave colonists found their final rest in shallow graves in the frost-bitten, uncharitable earth.

Could he have had a prophetic dream, this self-controlled, conservative Frenchman, that someday his settlement would be a city? Assuredly he could never have dreamed it would someday be a mecca for thousands because of the history he made there; he could never have imagined a sumptuous hotel on the site where he struggled to build a simple fort for which, after fours years, he still needed material even as his men needed food. The deterioration of the building had not been repaired in his absence, and as if it, like the men who had built it, lacked the strength to remain upright, one of the towers collapsed on July 9th, 1628.[7]

That summer, in July, news was brought to the harassed Lieutenant of the King of France that an English flotilla under Louis and Thomas Kirke was at Tadoussac with marauding intent.[8] The people were not kept long in suspense for a boat soon rounded the bend of the river at the corner of the Island of Orleans. As it landed below the habitation, it was seen to contain two envoys from the main fleet and several prisoners whom Kirke had already taken in his capture of the little settlement at Cap Tourmente.

In the name of the King of England and Commander Kirke, the envoys demanded that Champlain surrender his post to them. Since he was daily, almost hourly, expecting ships from France, Champlain abruptly and proudly refused, putting on so bold a front that the Englishmen were led to believe (as he intended them to be) that Quebec was in a position to defend herself for an indefinite period of time.

It seems odd that Kirke was so easily convinced of this. Possibly the impregnable appearance of the location and the knowledge he had gained of its strength daunted him, for, shortly after his envoys returned to him, he weighed anchor and sailed out of the harbour at Tadoussac.

[7]This is the date given by Dr. James Douglas in *Old France in the New World.*

[8]J. M. Le Moine gives the date of Kirke's arrival before Quebec as July 10th, 1628. P. G. Roy gives it as August 10th, 1628. Dr. James Douglas says it was the same day as the collapse of the tower which (he says) was July 9th, 1628.

But this was not to be the end of the annoyance he caused Champlain. No sooner had the English fleet emerged into the Gulf of St. Lawrence than it met the incoming French ships under de Roquemont. A fierce battle lasting fifteen hours ensued, ending with the capitulation of the French ships and resulting in greater scarcity of food and supplies for Quebec! The French ships, although armed for protection in this time of war, were not prepared for direct engagement with a fleet. They were heavily laden, had none too many soldiers aboard and little ammunition.

For the time being, quite satisfied with their victory and believing the colony of Quebec would be an easier prey a little later due to starvation, the English sailed triumphantly home.

The winter of 1628-29 was but a more painful repetition of previous winters. Did Champlain ever doubt that New France would prove worthy of the cruel sacrifices and hardships she de-demanded? The need for food exceeded everything; the settlers now lived mostly on dried peas and roots. They sold some of their much needed clothing to the Indians for smoked eels. Hunting was poor in the woods, not only because the hunters were in constant danger of being scalped by the Indians, but because the snow was deeper than ever before . Hunger dulled all ambition, stifled courage, weakened the desire to labour, and blinded the eyes to the beauty of the landscape.

Spring brought hope — but no ships.

Simultaneously with the fall of another of the towers of the Fort in the summer of 1629,[9] the English fleet under Louis Kirke again appeared in the harbour of Quebec, imperatively demanding the surrender of the post. This time Champlain had no choice but to capitulate; had he possessed a sufficient number of fit men, a reasonable amount of ammunition and food, he would have stood his ground, but after a few days of bombardment from the English,[10] he realized it would be useless.

There must have been despair and bitterness in the heart of Champlain as he sat in his humble habitation for the last time (he had not yet occupied Fort St. Louis) and penned the

[9]J. M. Le Moine gives the date as July 19th, 1629.
[10]Henry Kirke in *The First English Conquest of Canada,* (1871).

words that gave Quebec to the English: bitterness against his King for failing to realize that this country of fruitful soil was a land worth having: and despair for all the years of labour and planning and sacrifice which now were nothing but a prize for an enemy. And so he wrote the following words of capitulation:

"19th July, 1629.

> Gentlemen,
>
> It is too true, that owing to the want of succours and assistance from France, that our distress is very great, and that we are incapable of resistance—I therefore desire, that you will not fire on the town, nor land your troops, until the Articles of Capitulation can be drawn up."

On July 22nd, 1629,[11] the grief-stricken inhabitants watched the fleur-de-lis drop down from its place above the Fort St. Louis to be replaced by the conqueror's ensign.[12] Champlain bore himself nobly as his captors escorted him, two days later, to one of their ships bound for England. On every side he saw those true friends and co-sufferers, whom he would have died to protect, being left behind in the hands of the enemy.[13]

It is said to the credit of the English that, although they robbed him of his heart's treasure, they treated Champlain with every courtesy and consideration, and upon his arrival in England permitted him every freedom. A few months later he was allowed to return to France.

During the three years of English rule, no progress whatever was made in the settlement of Quebec or on its buildings. The conquerors under the command of Louis Kirke finished the Fort St. Louis sufficiently to make it habitable, using it as their headquarters, but they made no improvements, nor any effort to colonize the country, nor to convert the Indians. In fact, they had very little interest in this outpost on the rim of civilization. They suffered intensely from the winter climate, from lack of good food, and from disease. Out of a garrison of ninety, more than a tenth died that first winter. England, it appeared, had quickly grown tired of her prize and now scarcely knew what to do with it. An excuse for

[11]Dr. James Douglas, *Old France in the New World.*

[12]Probably the Union Flag of Queen Anne, or the Additional Jack of James I.

[13]Henry Kirke says, "Champlain surrendered Quebec to the English on the 9th of August, 1629."

this attitude may be found in the fact that England's internal troubles were fast leading to Civil War.

On his return to France, Champlain was re-united with Marie-Hélène, only to be once more presented with the final fruits of his conversion of this young Huguenot girl. She steadfastly begged his permission to enter a convent. Champlain refused. Was he hoping that someday she would follow him again to Quebec?

On March 29th, 1632, the Treaty of St. Germain-en-Laye was signed by the English and French, and New France thereby once more became the property of her Motherland.

In the following summer[14] Emery de Caen reclaimed Quebec in the name of the King of France, and once more the fleur-de-lis was unfurled from the Fort St. Louis. The English departed the same day in ships laden with furs and other valuable stock.

The Habitation was in ashes, reportedly burned down upon being struck by lightning. The monasteries of the Jesuits and Recollets were bare, having been stripped of their belongings by the English. Broken windows stared like reproachful eyes, and doors whined desolately on rusty hinges. The gardens were overgrown with weeds.

In May of the following year (1633), Champlain returned, this time holding the title of Governor of all New France.

Deep and happy emotion stirred the settlers as they welcomed back their beloved leader. As he once more strode up the narrow roads between their houses they greeted him fervently, forming a retinue to accompany him to the church to give thanks to God for his safe return to them, and for their deliverance from the hands of the enemy.

At last Champlain took up his residence in the Fort St. Louis. But Marie-Hélène was not by his side. He was never to see her again. Even so, his personal loneliness did not make him less grateful to God for the restoration of New France. In his gratitude, he set to work at once to build a chapel to the Virgin which was thereafter known as the Church of Our Lady of the Restoration.

[14]Francis Parkman, in *Pioneers of France in the New World,* gives the date as July 5, 1632.
P. G. Roy, in *La Ville de Québec sous le Régime Français,* agrees with Parkman.
N. E. Dionne, in *Samuel Champlain,* gives the date as July 13, 1632.
J. M. Le Moine, *Quebec, Past and Present,* agrees with Dr. Dionne.

This edifice, burned in 1640, is said by some to have stood where the English Cathedral now stands; by others, to have been replaced by the church that has since become the present Basilica.

During the next year or two Quebec developed into a busy trading post. The old Company of France, known as the Company of the One Hundred Associates, which had handled colonization so badly, was dissolved and the charter given to a group which, fortunately for Canada, was prompted by religion and patriotism instead of greed and selfishness. More ships appeared yearly in the port that now boasted a few crude wharves. Most Indian tribes, with the exception of the Iroquois and their confederates, made their way to the settlement to barter their furs for such trinkets as they had never known existed. Conversion among them met with a measure of success, but Champlain was far from satisfied with it and was tireless in his efforts to spread Christianity.

New buildings were springing up everywhere as more colonists arrived. Gradually the paths between the houses took the form of the winding streets that are today one of Quebec's most charming characteristics.

By this time Champlain was nearing his sixty-eighth birthday. His activities had necessarily become less strenuous and he devoted much of his time to the conversion of the savages and in the writing of his descriptive journals. He had always lived a pious and noble life, courageous in every respect; had accomplished what few would have attempted; had made great personal sacrifices for the sake of New France; and had never spared himself in the service of others.

"Fort St. Louis was like a school of religion and every virtue," says Dr. Dionne.[15] "They lived there as in a monastery. There was a lecture during meals; in the morning they read history, and at supper the lives of the saints. Afterwards they said their prayers, and Champlain had introduced the old French custom of ringing the church bells three times a day, during recitation of the *Angelus*. At night, everyone was invited to go to Champlain's room for the night's prayer, said by Champlain himself."

[15] *Samuel Champlain.*

But now he was growing old. His role in the great drama of founding a nation was almost over; soon he must bow out and leave the stage to others. Someone else must find that elusive route to China. In mid-October, 1635, he was stricken helpless with paralysis; death seemed but a matter of days or, at most, a few weeks. He was so ill as to be unable to sign his will. For two and a half months, the intrepid explorer lay stricken in the Fort St. Louis before death released him on Christmas day.

The colonists were stunned and sorrowful. Their love for their leader and protector was deep and genuine. It was an enormous loss for which there seemed no earthly compensation. At the burial service in the chapel he had so lovingly built, every honour was accorded the great man. The colony, joined by hundreds of Champlain's Indian converts, gathered to pay humble tribute to a beloved friend.

****

When the news reached France, Marie-Hélène wept her husband's passing as she knelt at a candle-lit altar. She knew that he now would understand her desire to take herself from the world. Some time later, as soon as her affairs and those of her late husband could be settled,[16] she entered the Ursuline convent at Faubourg St. Jacques where she became a novice and took the name of *Sister Hélène de St. Augustin.* Three years later (1648) she founded another such convent at Meaux into which she retired after making a public confession of her faults, kneeling, with a lighted candle in her hand, and wearing a cord about her neck. She remained in the convent until her death on December 20th, 1654, at the age of fifty.

The story of the *Sieur de Champlain* and his lady is one for reflection. Was his love for New France greater than his love for her? Was her desire to serve God in a cloister greater than her

[16]This was not an easy matter. Their marriage settlement had stated that Champlain would, at his death, leave all his possessions to his wife. In his will he named the Virgin Mary as his sole heir, doubtless believing that Madame de Champlain would approve. However, it was not she who contested the will but a first cousin of Champlain, Madame Marie Camaret Hersault, wife of the Comptroller of Customs at La Rochelle. This famous trial decided the will was authentic but ordered that it be set aside. Consequently, all but nine hundred livres of his estate were given to the natural heirs. (N. E. Dionne in *Samuel Champlain.* Makers of Canada Series.)

desire to serve her husband in a restless New World? . . . . Perhaps if the home on the mountain had been blessed with earlier success, the story would have ended differently.

****

In 1898, two hundred and sixty-three years after the death of Champlain, there was erected a monument worthy of him on the esplanade between the Château Frontenac and the brow of the cliff where his fort had once stood. His figure stands high on a Doric pedestal; he faces inland, doffing his plumed hat in salute to the New World; in the other hand is his commission from Henry IV of France, bearing the seal and *fleur-de-lis.* From base to crown the height of the monument is fifty feet, the figure alone being fourteen feet nine inches. It was designed by Cardonnel of Paris and sculptured by Chevré.

The smaller figures at the base of this monument are interesting. A woman, representing the City of Quebec, is inscribing in the book of immortality the name of the founder of the city. On her right is a child, the Genius of Navigation, denoting the profession of Champlain. Above these figures is a small angel with outspread wings proclaiming the glory of the man. In the upper section of the pedestal are found the Arms of Brouage, the birthplace of Champlain; of Quebec, where he lived and died; and of Canada, who claims him as one of her immortals.

The monument was unveiled on September 21st, 1898, in the presence of dignitaries, Church, State and Military, with Lord Aberdeen, then Governor-General of Canada, officiating.

But Canada itself is a truer monument to Champlain than ever one of stone can be . . . .

****

Chapter Two

THE FIRST CHÂTEAU in the New World was erected during the next twelve years by Champlain's successor, the Chevalier Charles Huault de Montmagny. Though not an elaborate building, it was of ambitious and noble proportions, in accord with Montmagny's character of severest simplicity. Begun in 1647, and located within the enclosure of the fortifications built by Champlain, this first Château St. Louis had four towers and a balcony, and was supported by stone buttresses. Today, hidden by Dufferin Terrace and the Château Frontenac, these buttresses are all that remain of the first castle in Canada.

The new Governor also reinforced the fortifications with sand and limestone, and built a rampart of oak and cedar on that side of the château which is now Place d'Armes.

Governor Montmagny was fanatically pious; he was a Knight of the ancient Order of St. John of Malta, or Knights Hospitallers. He observed its rules of obedience, poverty and chastity throughout his life, attaining before his death in 1654 the rank of Commander of the Order. With him at Quebec were four of his brother Knights: Antoine de Bréhaut de l'Isle, who accompanied him to New France as his lieutenant; Bras-de-Fer de Châteaufort, who had administered the affairs of the government of New France for the short period between Champlain's death and Montmagny's arrival; Noel Brulart de Sillery, who later became a priest and founded that section of Quebec known as Sillery; and the Sieur Isaac de Razilly, a naval officer, a foremost member of the Company of the Knights Hospitallers.

Extremely zealous on behalf of his beloved Order, and for wealth and power for it, Montmagny was also not averse to any personal prestige that might be gained thereby. He eventually drew upon himself the displeasure of his King whose cause he had promised to serve above all else; the King considered that Montmagny's activities on behalf of the Order were interfering with the interests of the Crown. Royal disapproval soon made itself felt among the knights of Quebec; from this time, the Order declined in New France.

But while the Order was in its heyday in the New World the Brothers had every intention of building a Priory for themselves in Quebec. Various historians have referred to this Priory; some claim it was never completed; others that it was destroyed early in the siege of Quebec in 1759. Nevertheless, a very real and tangible proof exists today that Montmagny had faith that they would have a Priory in Quebec. He had a stone carved with the Cross of Malta upon it and the date, 1647; doubtless with the intention of placing it on the wall of the Priory when it should be built.

Today this stone has a place of honour in the outer wall of the Château Frontenac, where all may see it and speculate upon its origin and history. Beneath it has been added the simple inscription:

Stone carved for the Priory of
the Knights of Malta, Quebec, 1647.

The Cross of Malta, which has the appearance of four arrowheads meeting at their points, was the symbol of an organization first founded in 1048 by a group of Italian merchants for the protection of the sick and destitute pilgrims to the Holy Land. Its purpose then was wholly secular but, after the Crusades, during which the Knights cared for the sick and wounded, the organization became a religious Order and adopted a uniform consisting of a plain black robe with the eight-pointed Maltese Cross in white linen affixed to the left side of the breast. In 1118, these Knights Hospitallers, as they called themselves, were composed of three classes: the first were men of noble ancestry and military distinction; the second were priests; the third were serving-men.

For over a hundred years the Knights maintained a military character by fighting the enemies of Christianity, until they had captured the city of Rhodes where they resided until the beginning of the sixteenth century. Hence the title often given them: Knights of Rhodes. In 1522 they were compelled to leave Rhodes, which was forcefully taken from them by the Turks. In 1530, the Emperor of Germany gave them the little island of Malta, which they made their headquarters for two-hundred and sixty-eight years. Thus the title: Knights of Malta. In 1798 they were compelled to surrender their island to the French. From this date, the Order declined until today there is no organization in existence that is connected with the glorious Knights of Malta.

In 1885, the Quebec *Morning Chronicle* carried a series of letters from its readers on the matter of the origin of the Malta Stone. Colonel R. E. Carr of Worcester, England (who had recently visited Canada and become interested in the early history of Quebec, in particular the Malta Stone) had written his friend Major Dennis Murray, Clerk of the Peace of Quebec, regarding the origin of the Stone. Upon publication of these letters, Mr. J. M. Le Moine,* historian, and Mr. E. T. D. Chambers, an editorial writer of the *Chronicle,* each contributed their opinions on the stone. The controversy hinged upon an article which had appeared in the Italian-American *Gazetteer* of Leghorn, as long ago as 1763. Each had his opinion as to whether the Order had had a Priory in Quebec and whether the Stone had been upon it or upon the Château St. Louis when Montmagny built it in 1647.

The extract from the *Gazetteer* read[1]:

"The city is well built, and full of superb edifices, such as churches and palaces; but there are especially the palace of the Bishop, the Tribunals of Justice, the House of Knights of Jerusalem, which is a superb building of square stones, and which is said to have cost £40,000 sterling; with convents of friars, monks, chapels, etc., which it would occupy too much time to describe. But the most notable edifice of all is the Palace (of St. Louis), where the Governor resides, in which was the Grand Council of Carolina, when Quebec was in the hands of the French, and where were kept all the Royal archives."

Mr. Chambers wrote: "It is scarcely probable that a chapter house at Quebec for the Knights of St. John was furnished by the Government of France, and it is therefore more reasonable to suppose that the Quebec Priory of 1647 assembled for their chapter meetings in an apartment fitted up for their reception either in the Château or in the Fort St. Louis. That neither the members of the Order in New France, nor its head in Europe, could afford

*Later Sir James M. Le Moine.

[1]This excerpt is taken from *The History of The Knights Templars of Canada,* by J. Ross Robertson. (Toronto: Hunter, Rose & Co., 1890)

the necessary sum for the erection of a house in Quebec, is evident from the letter to de Razilly, already referred to,[2] and from which it appears that on account of the costly fortifications then being made at Malta, the Grand Master, though fully appreciating the foreign labours of his correspondent, was regretfully compelled to express his inability to send him any financial aid." Mr. Chambers further adds that possibly the writer of the article in the Italian-American *Gazetteer* (which had been translated from the English and published in Italian) had seen the Maltese Cross on the wall of the Château St. Louis and had concluded that that wall had once formed a part of the Priory for the Knights of St. John of Malta.

Mr. Le Moine,[3] to whom everyone listened with great respect said: "I am in possession of a short note from the learned Abbé Bois, F.R.S.C., which corroborates the position taken by the Levis antiquarian,[4] from which I quote the following: 'The Knights of St. John of Jerusalem, established at Quebec,—Bras-de-Fer, Montmagny, Sillery, etc.,—had erected a *bureau* in the yard of the Castle St. Louis; it cost 40,000 livres (not pounds) of French money. The gable contained a large stone, set in the wall, on which was engraved the arms of the Order. This stone having dropped to the ground when the edifice was destroyed by fire in July, 1759, (during the early days of the siege), remained amongst the ruins until 1784, when the military force detailed to level the lot found it and placed it in the wall of the Chateau yard. The shield was carried to England, and after knocking about in the public stores, it was placed at . . . . I have the whole particulars among my papers but I am too ill to look them up. (Signed) L. E. Bois'."

In the course of the argument, an extract from the Journals of Captain John Knox, who had been at the siege of Quebec, was quoted. In describing the buildings of Quebec after the capitula-

[2]Of this letter, Mr. Chambers said, "it was addressed to de Razilly on Feb. 20, 1636, by the Grand Master of the Knights of St. John of Jerusalem, and which those interested may read for themselves at page 114, Vol. I, of the *Documents Historiques relatifs à la Nouvelle France*, recently published (1883) by the Provincial Government under the personal supervision of Hon. Jean Blanchet, Provincial Secretary."

[3]*See footnote p. 26.*

[4]Joseph Edmund Roy, distinguished historian.

tion of Quebec to the English in 1759, Knox makes mention of the "stately but unfinished house for the Knights Hospitallers". In this connection it is well to note the reference made to it by Mr. P. G. Roy in his book, *La Ville de Québec Sous le Régime Français,* in which he remarks that the Hôtel Dieu was, in 1759, an "unfinished house"; possibly Knox had been confused.

In the same book, Mr. Roy gives the French version of a letter allegedly written by the Abbé Bois: "Les chevaliers de Saint-Jean de Jerusalem, établis à Québec, Bras-de-Fer, Montmagny, Sillery, etc., avaient construit un bureau dans la cour du château Saint-Louis. Il avait coûté 40,000 livres, de la monnaie française. Une grande pierre, incrustée dans le mur de façade portait les armes de l'ordre. Quand l'édifice fut détruit par le feu, en juillet 1759, pendant le siège, cette pierre fut enfouie sous les ruines jusqu'en 1784. En cette année, les autorités militaires en firent l'invention et la placérent dans le mur de la cour du château."

If we assume that the Priory was never completed—(if it was, it has yet to be proven beyond doubt)—where did Montmagny place his stone? Is it not highly probable that he placed it over the gateway, or in the wall, of the château which he was building at that time, especially if the chapter meetings of the Order were held there? Or was it by using it as a cornerstone of the château that he incurred the displeasure of his King who undoubtedly considered that a stone bearing the Royal arms would have been much more fitting?

Although Abbé Bois says the Malta Stone fell among the ruins in 1759, there is no proof that it was still in existence at that time. The Abbé was most certainly not there to have seen it prior to the siege. No one else records it as having been lost in 1759. Is it not possible that it had been lost before then? That when the Comte de Frontenac undertook to rebuild Montmagny's château in 1684, the extensive repairs carried on may have resulted in the disappearance of the Stone? In this case, it remained hidden for a span of ninety years. In 1784, the Building Supervisor,[5] James Thompson, a former sergeant in Wolfe's Army at the time of the battle for Quebec in 1759, (and of whom we learn more later), recorded the discovery of the Malta Stone in his diary,

[5]or, Superintendent of Works.

accompanying it with a rough drawing of it:

"1784, September 17th,

The miners at the Chateau, in levelling the yard dug up a large stone which I have described in the annexed figure. I could wish it was discovered soon enough to lay conspicuously in the wall of the new building in order to convey to posterity the antiquity of the Castle of Saint-Louis; however, I got the masons to lay the stone in the cheek of the gate of the new building."

The "new building" to which Mr. Thompson alludes was the Château Haldimand (later to be known as the Old Château, or le Vieux Château), which was at that time in process of erection by Sir Frederick Haldimand, then Governor-General of Canada under British Rule. It was situated very near the Château St. Louis.

In 1892, when it was first proposed to erect a massive hotel on the site of the Château St. Louis, and it was found necessary to demolish the Château Haldimand, the ancient panel bearing the Maltese Cross was carefully preserved. In the lease of the property, on which the Old Château stood, to the Château Frontenac Company, there was a stipulation that this relic should be set in some prominent place on the wall of the new hotel.

Today, effaced as it is with the wear of three hundred years, during which the date on the original carving has been worn away leaving only the Cross, with its mystery still unrevealed, this Stone holds a place of distinction on the equally famous château that the good Montmagny built in 1647. Set in the keystone of the entrance archway of the Château Frontenac (on the inner—or courtyard—side where it would suffer less weathering), this old Stone looks down benevolently on the people of a new age.

✻✻✻✻✻✻✻✻✻✻✻✻

Governor Montmagny was a worthy successor to the first Governor of New France. His goodness and kindness were a shining example to those about him. Upon his arrival in Quebec on June 11th, 1636, he had proceeded to the church at once for a special Mass, an act symbolic of the twelve years of his stay in New France. There is a legend[6] which tells that he fell spontan-

[6]This legend is recorded by J. B. A. Ferland in *Cours d'Histoire du Canada,* (1861) and by Dr. William Kingsford in *History of Canada,* Vol. I.

eously to his knees when, as he was ascending the hill to the fort immediately after his disembarkation, a rough cross came in sight. Legend further adds that the cross marked the grave of Champlain. The Jesuit Fathers tell us that Montmagny would permit no special service to be offered him in church, that he always knelt with the humblest of the people to receive the Sacrament.

Though a peaceful man by nature, Montmagny was a soldier, and therefore it was natural that, upon becoming aware of the Indian situation in New France, he should consider it advisable (as did Champlain) to solidify the friendship then existing between the French and the Huron and Algonquin tribes. He petitioned France for soldiers and ammunition and made a detailed statement of Quebec's needs to be presented to the King. The Royal reply was, as ever, evasive and unsatisfactory, producing little result.

Under Montmagny's régime, much material progress was made in the colony of Quebec. New buildings were erected with more order in their location than before; roads were laid out according to plans drawn up by the Governor, and the work was done under his supervision. Thus, St. Louis street, and its extension, Grande Allée, came into being, thereby marking Quebec City forever with the impress of the noble and wise Montmagny.

He succeeded, too, in obtaining permission from the Company of the Hundred Associates for the inhabitants to trade in furs, a privilege heretofore denied them.

The influence of this Governor's austere life was obvious in his château, and was felt by all who had occasion to go there. Religious relics adorned its walls; the furniture was simple and sparse; and there was no ornamentation but a few tapestries depicting the glories of the Knights Hospitallers. The rooms were habitually peopled with priests with whom the Governor was always in closest association. No social functions of any description were ever held there. No women ever graced its halls—in fact, there were few in Quebec—to mingle a brighter costume with the sober garb of knight and priest.

During the twelfth year of his governorship Montmagny was recalled. The King of France belatedly decided to take an interest in New France and one of his first acts was to limit the term of a governor of New France to three years. Montmagny left Quebec on September 23rd, 1648. He died at St. Christophe in 1654.

The governors immediately succeeding the Chevalier Montmagny left no lasting mark, as he did, upon the Fort and Château St. Louis or upon the rapidly growing town of Quebec.

Louis d'Ailleboust de Coulonge arrived in Quebec from Montreal on August 20th, 1648, accompanied by his wife, the former Marie-Barbe de Boulogne, and her sister, Philippine. D'Ailleboust had come to New France in 1643,[7] in command of a detachment for Montreal. His services had been warmly welcomed there by the Sieur de Maisonneuve, Governor of Montreal, as he possessed invaluable knowledge of construction engineering and he was at once set the task of overseeing the improvements on the fortifications of Montreal.

With the arrival of the d'Aillebousts' in Quebec, the colony seemed to develop more normally with a nucleus of social life centred in the Château St. Louis, that was more than welcome. Madame d'Ailleboust was a bright and charming creature, and the monastic Château quickly showed the effect of a woman presiding graciously over its well-being.

Notwithstanding the sociality of the Governor and his wife, they were extremely religious. Madame d'Ailleboust's sister, Philippine, had entered the Ursuline Convent immediately upon her arrival in Quebec, and this seemed to inspire Marie-Barbe with a longing to do likewise in spite of the fact that she had a husband. She had been deeply devout all her life. In her early girlhood she had made a vow of eternal chastity which influenced her as long as she lived. Although she was married to M. d'Ailleboust, he was under threat of stern retribution should he cause her to break her vow. "God will chastise you terribly," said the Jesuit who married them, to d'Ailleboust, "if you forget the promise you have made."[8] Consequently, they lived like monk and nun, and this unusual woman and her equally unusual husband remained utterly faithful to their vows.[9]

[7]Some historians say that Madame d'Ailleboust and her sister did not come to New France until 1644, that M. d'Ailleboust came in 1643 to bring a detachment to Montreal.

[8]". . . si vous oubliez la promesse que vous lui faites . . . . Dieu vous châtiera terriblement," as related by Mother Juchereau de Saint-Ignace. (P. G. Roy, in *La Ville de Québec sous le Régime Français.*) [9]P. G. Roy. *Op. Cit.*

Marie-Barbe d'Ailleboust actually did enter the convent in Quebec during her husband's lifetime but, after a month's trial, she gave it up and resumed her place as the first lady of the first vice-regal court in Canada, and the leader of Quebec's small and disciplined society.

Like the men who had gone before him, d'Ailleboust was keenly interested in the conversion of the Indians and never for a moment relaxed his efforts in this direction. Although he wished only to lead a quiet and peaceful existence, the Iroquois gave him little opportunity to do so; they waxed fiercer than ever in their efforts to wipe out the white man or to drive him back to the land whence he came. It was at this time that civil war between the tribes of Hurons and Iroquois had all but exterminated the weaker Huron tribe, and the remnants of it had settled their wigwam villages on the slopes and in the fields around Quebec in the hope of protection and sustenance from the white man. Today, three centuries later, their descendants are found in a reservation at Lorette, eight miles from the city of Quebec.

The Royal court of France seemed once more to have lost interest in its colonial offspring. D'Ailleboust repeatedly requested that a garrison be sent out from France; but, as usual, the requests were disregarded. Progress in the colony was nullified by the incessant attacks of the savages. The Governor realized how absolutely the people relied upon his resourcefulness, and, knowing he possessed all too little, tried to form an alliance with the New England colonies to the south against the Iroquois. He failed miserably.

At the end of his three-year term of office, d'Ailleboust retired to Montreal and was replaced in Quebec by M. Jean de Lauzon who held the office of governor for five years (inconsistent with the new ruling that a governor should hold office for three years only), and then, when it was no longer to his advantage, he relinquished it.

De Lauzon was a different type of man to his predecessors. It was obvious from the time of his arrival on October 14th, 1651.[10] He was a widower with three sons who completely filled his life. His efforts to get them married to wealthy or distinguished girls caused considerable undesirable gossip in Quebec and Mont-

[10]This is the date given by Dr. William Kingsford, in *History of Canada,* Vol. I.

real. He succeeded in the cases of two of his sons, who married into gratifyingly aristocratic families. Not content with this, de Lauzon began to create, upon his own authority, ridiculous, high-sounding titles for his sons. The second son, de Charny, was made "Grand Maître des Eaux et Forêts". The Governor then acquired, by scarcely irreproachable means, large tracts of land for himself and his family. The Seigneury of Lauzon, now a small but prosperous town adjoining the city of Levis, across the St. Lawrence River from the city of Quebec, still retains his name. Farther afield, he established a trading depot at Tadoussac for his own especial commercial operations and caused ill-feeling among the inhabitants by refusing them its privileges. By such means did this Governor add to his unpopularity.

Finally becoming aware of the extent of the disfavour he had incurred, and being unable to cope in any respect with the Iroquois hordes, since he was himself too old to head the troops under his command, de Lauzon abruptly shifted the cares of State to the shoulders of his son, M. de Charny. After continuing in his father's steps for a short time, de Charny suffered the death of his wife and he thereupon relinquished his position to M. Louis d'Ailleboust of Montreal, and betook himself to France where he subsequently entered the priesthood.

It is indeed peculiar that Jean de Lauzon should have discharged his duties as governor so weakly. He had been the Company's Intendent in France before coming to New France and was well-versed in its affairs. And yet, during the five years of his governorship, everything was at a standstill in Quebec awaiting gubernatorial direction. That it was not forthcoming is evidence of the self-centered nature of the man. He returned to France, where he died on February 16th, 1666.

By the time M. d'Ailleboust obligingly resumed the reins—presumably for a few weeks until a new governor should be appointed, but actually for a year—the colony was in greater danger than ever from the Indians. The red men had sensed the weakness that existed within the Château St. Louis. It seemed to be their cue for concerted onslaughts. Once again the soil of Quebec, where now are soft green lawns, parks, wide streets and narrow streets, was drenched with the blood of those simple honest forefathers who sought only to make a living and to worship God in their chosen way.

In 1648 the Fort St. Louis was garrisoned by a dozen soldiers together with what was known as "a flying squadron of forty men for actice field service" — which probably meant sorties against the savages. To his great credit, d'Ailleboust left no measures untried to make peace with the Indians. In the month of May, 1658, he invited the chieftains, or their deputies, to assemble in the Château St. Louis to listen to discourses and harangues on the benefits of civilization and Christianity under French rule. A large number of Indians accepted this official invitation, which promised at the same time to end with an elegant feast. During the proceedings, many—too many indeed!—stood on the great gallery of the château that overlooked the river. The gallery, like the rest of the Château St. Louis, was suffering from disrepair, and the number of persons milling restlesly upon it proved too much of a strain. With a great creaking of timber and crumbling of stone, it gave way and precipitated all the guests into a heap outside the château. It is said that no one was badly hurt; however, though every attempt was made to carry the meeting to its conclusion, it does not surprise one to learn that any friendly feelings the Indians might tentatively have held for the French were not improved by such unceremonious treatment so damaging to the dignity.

D'Ailleboust was released from his temporary governorship of Quebec on July 11th, 1658, and he returned once more to Montreal where he died on May 31st, 1660.

After her husband's death, the lively Marie-Barbe d'Ailleboust again entered a convent as a novice, remaining a year. Then, finally admitting her unsuitability for the life, she retired to the Hôtel Dieu of Quebec and lived like a saint, and the Château St. Louis saw her no more. It is said that she received proposals of marriage from such esteemed and likable gentlemen as Governor de Courcelles and the Intendant Talon,[11] who both came to Canada a few years after d'Ailleboust's death. She died on June 7th, 1685, at the age of seventy, and was buried in the Hôtel Dieu[12], beside the nuns whom she loved.

[11]P. G. Roy in *La Ville de Québec sous le Régime Français.*

[12]". . . elle fut inhumée à l'Hôtel Dieu . . . à côté des bonnes religieuses qu'elle aimait tant." P. G. Roy. *Op. Cit.*

Chapter Three

DURING THE NEXT fourteen years, six good and noble gentlemen undertook to guide the destiny of New France, and the Château St. Louis formed only a vague—albeit graceful—backdrop for the affairs that marked the era of Canadian history that was to be known as the "heroic age".

The period is marked by the appearance of Francis Xavier de Montmorency-Laval, Bishop of Petrea, a man of dominant personality, who brooked no interference or opposition to his ruling, and who favoured extreme measures for the advancement of the Holy Cause. All his life he rigidly practised self-denial and seemed pitilessly devoid of understanding of the errors of those human beings who did not possess the strength to control themselves likewise; who had not passed their whole lives in pious learning and had not attained that state of perfection wherein are no weaknesses, errors or omissions.

One by one the six gentlemen of state—d'Argenson, d'Avaugour, de Mezy, de Tracy, de Courcelles, Talon—passed beneath the rod of this all-powerful prelate; one by one each learned his lesson, meekly or rebelliously, as Bishop Laval would have him know it. As the years rolled by it seemed as if their lives were so completely filled with this antagonistic struggle of wills (for so it became) that there was little if any time for the pleasantries and gaiety that might have enlivened the stern simplicity of the Château St. Louis. Sadly missed were the delicate touch and gracious kindly presence of Madame d'Ailleboust—and no one came to replace her.

Even the Indian warfare, with its perilous significance, seemed a minor matter beside the conflict that possessed the powers for good in New France.

Pierre de Voyer, Vicomte d'Argenson, was appointed Governor of New France on January 26th, 1657, and landed in Quebec on July 11th, 1658, after two attempts to cross the sea, during which his ship twice ran aground off the Irish coast. He was a young man in his early thirties, an officer with a distinguished military record, well-educated, of kindly disposition and good sense.

M. de'Ailleboust, who had not yet departed for Montreal, awaited the Vicomte's arrival at the dockside on that warm July morning. After greeting the newcomer with every courtesy, he escorted him with due ceremony up Mountain Hill (the rough path had by this time become a well-worn corduroy road), to the Château St. Louis. On every side were crowds of people shouting their welcome; bunting was hung from the windows of the houses, and cannon boomed a salute from the Fort. At the portal of the Fort, d'Ailleboust formally presented d'Argenson with its keys.

Scarcely had d'Argenson refreshed himself within the cool halls of the Château, than his Lieutenant hastily summoned him with the news that the Iroquois were murdering the peaceful Algonquins who had encamped on the slopes of Cape Diamond. With a quick grasp of the situation—admirable for one so new to his position and so ignorant of prevailing conditions—the new Governor despatched a force to the rescue. It is said that he himself led the force that drove back the intruders.[1]

As soon as he had had a chance to investigate the state of the colony, d'Argenson made a report to the Company of New France whose headquarters were in the homeland, begging for more troops, insisting that the only way to save the colony from being annihilated by the Iroquois was to wage an offensive war upon them. He had, as he advised the Company, only one hundred men to defend Quebec against twenty-four hundred Indians. The Company's answer, though of gratifying length, was that the Governor's chief concern should not be the waging of an offensive war but the collecting of furs now long overdue the Company from the inhabitants in return for the privilege it had granted them of trading in furs.

D'Argenson had been in New France nearly a year when Bishop Laval arrived. At first they were well disposed toward each other—indeed, they had no reason to be otherwise. D'Argenson was a sincere Catholic and a man of worth and dignity. But before long trouble broke out between them. Neither could agree upon the other's power of jurisdiction in matters both political and ecclesiastical. Laval believed he had supreme power in Can-

[1]P. G. Roy, *La Ville de Québec sous le Régime Français.*

ada and was responsible only to the Pope. D'Argenson believed his position as Governor-in-chief of all New France gave him the privilege of interfering in matters ecclesiastic if he chose to do so. In short, each considered himself in the right, acting according to the authority invested in him by his superior.

D'Argenson was sorely troubled, too, over money matters. In a letter to a friend in France, he wrote: "The costs of living here are horrible. I have only 2,000 crowns a year for all my expenses and I have already been compelled to go into debt to the Company for an equal amount."

Young as he was, d'Argenson could endure the conditions no longer than the required three years. In 1661, he wrote to France for his recall. His nerves were frayed from constant bickering with the Bishop, from worry over finances, from concern over the safety of the colony, and from sheer disgust at the neglect of its interests by the Company. His health began to suffer. "I see no reason," he wrote, "for staying here any longer. When I came to this country, I hoped to enjoy a little repose but I am doubly deprived of it, on the one hand by enemies without and incessant petty disputes within, and on the other hand by the difficulty I have in subsisting."

D'Argenson was noted for his insistence upon etiquette and convention at all times, under all circumstances, maintaining his court in Quebec in the manner he considered ethical. Little wonder he was concerned over the Company's neglect. They granted him no money for the upkeep and maintenance of the Fort and Château St. Louis, and so it fell into a disgraceful condition. An inventory of the buildings there, drawn up by Simon Denys, Procurer-General of the Company of New France, dated the last day of September, 1660, proves that the Viscount was justified in despairing of the fate of the colony. Says M. Denys, "The gate of the fort is in ruins and out of use, the unfinished walls of the fort are in a similar state, the parapets totally ruined, the platform over the great door, where a sentry-box is located, is entirely in ruin, the great bastion on the west side, threatening to fall, has been demolished; the rampart over the great door, leading from the bastion to the sentry-box, which is on the north side, is entirely ruined; all the ladders and steps going up to the ramparts and the ammunition store are rotten and out of service, etc. . . ."[2]

D'Argenson's successor, the Baron du Bois d'Avaugour, arrived on August 31st, 1661. D'Argenson departed for France on September 19th.

From the first, d'Avaugour's consternation over the condition of the colony was but an echo of his predecessor, and he expressed profound surprise that the undertaking had not long ago been abandoned. The result of his cogitation on the state of affairs was the suggestion, made to his Colonial Minister, that New France should become a Royal province, to be treated with the same consideration. If this seed had but fallen on fruitful soil, it need not have waited two years to emerge.

D'Avaugour was nearer middle age than d'Argenson; he was of a more domineering nature, more dynamic and energetic, with an utter disregard for pomp and ostentation that was often embarrassing to his entourage. As soon as he learned of the festivities planned for his arrival in Quebec he ordered them cancelled. Thus the colony wondered what manner of man this new governor was even before he had set foot within the settlement.

During D'Avaugour's régime the State's chief difficulties with the Church (or vice-versa) were based on the question of selling brandy to the Indians. Although the new Governor was soon appraised of the evils attendant upon the sale of the "fiery liquid" to the savages and frowned upon it, he refused to agree with Bishop Laval that the offenders must be excommunicated, nor would he concur in the death sentence which Laval ultimately decreed for the transgressors.

But now there was to be divine intervention in the squabble—or so it seemed. This intervention took the form of that most terrifying of all geological phenomena — less understood then than now—an earthquake. And it brought the wicked to their knees as the Bishop could never have done. However, in view of the obsti-

[2]Denys is quoted by P. G. Roy in *La Ville de Québec Sous le Régime Français*: "la barrière du fort est ruine et hors de service, l'enceinte du fort de murs non achievés en état tel quel, les parapets totalement ruinés, la plate-form sur la grande porte où est assis une guérite le tout ruiné, le grand bastion du coté de l'ouest menaçant ruine a été démoli; le rempart passant sur la grande porte allant du bastion à la guérite qui est du coté du nord est entièrement ruiné; toutes les échelles et degrés servant à monter sur iceux remparts et dans le magasin des armes pourries et hors de service, etc., etc. . . ."

nacy which d'Avaugour had displayed in his dealings with the Bishop, it is to be doubted if the spectacle of destruction brought him to the point of bowing the knee (since he had not considered himself wrong) as it did the rest of the sinful little colony. As for the Bishop suffering qualms regarding the harshness of his measures, he was—perhaps fortunately for him—on a visit to France, and so missed the gratifying spectacle of dozens of his parishioners flocking to the church and the confessionals amid the upheaval.

D'Avaugour was present through it all and felt the shock rumble the rock upon which his château was situated. He saw it toss the ice-jammed waters of the St. Lawrence river until they raged like a storm at sea. He saw his furniture move of its own accord, and doors swing wildly to and fro; gusts of hot air laden with sand rattled the windows, and everywhere the air was stifling and oppressive. Outside, the very earth moved treacherously up and down; and bells rang in a hideous clamour only to be drowned by deafening claps of thunder that was like no thunder ever heard before. On all sides people ran frantically hither and yon, screaming, searching for loved ones, falling in despair upon their knees.

It was undoubtedly the vengeance of heaven upon a wicked people—or so the people believed.

In William Smith's *History of Canada* (1815), there is mention of the fort in connection with the earthquake—"the walls of the fortifications were rent"—but this seems to be the only reference made to its effect on the Fort or Château St. Louis.

And there was not only one terrible convulsion. It was followed, over a period of six or seven months, by thirty-two shocks[3] of varying intensity, as though heaven would further remind the people of the promises made on that memorable day of February 5th, 1663, when the first upheaval sent them to their knees. There were many in Quebec who remembered that year for many years thereafter, not only because of the shock it gave their consciences and their nerves, but for the struggle they had to rebuild the humble homes that had collapsed, to clear away the trees which the winds had uprooted and thrown across their gardens, and in searching for the few domestic animals that had taken to the woods in a

[3]Dr. William Kingsford in *History of Canada,* Vol. I.

frenzy of fear at every fresh tremor. Strangely enough, when the earth had finally settled back to normal some seven months or so later, it was found that the shocks had not caused a single death.

The Bishop's visit to France was in itself unpropitious so far as the recalcitrant Governor was concerned. Laval, having reached the limit of his clerical endurance over d'Avaugour's obstinacy, had gone to present to the Colonial Minister in person his request that the Governor be recalled. The ship that carried the Bishop back to Quebec also carried the document of d'Avaugour's recall.

To posterity, d'Avaugour seems to have been unusually unwise in some of his well-intentioned efforts to extend and enhance the power of France in the New World. He believed, for example, that it would be advantageous, for the Church as well as the Crown, to seize the apostate English territories of Boston and Manhattan. To accomplish this, he suggested (in a despatch to the Home government dated September 2nd, 1663), that he would need but four thousand men and ten ships. He further considered that it could be achieved in three months. The coveted territory contained, estimated the ill-advised Governor, about forty thousand men. This was an absurd understatement, as statistics show.

Although the procedure for conquest, as outlined by d'Avaugour, was certainly ambitious, it was also untimely since thousands of Indians had yet to be driven out of the immediate vicinity of Quebec—or converted to peaceful intentions. Fortunately for all concerned, the project received little consideration in France. It did, however, serve the excellent purpose of convincing the King that a little serious concern over this annoying community across the sea would not be amiss.

Upon investigation, King Louis' first step—and for it Canada and posterity owe him much—was to break up the Company of One Hundred Associates that had been effectively strangling all initiative in the whole of New France almost since its discovery. By an Edict, dated April, 1663, the King made New France a Royal province of his kingdom, and instituted a Sovereign Council for it along the lines of France's own Council of State. This was an important step in the direction advocated by d'Avaugour shortly after his arrival in Quebec. But many years were yet to pass before the seed he had planted in the Royal consciousness was to attain the fruition necessary to the progress of New France.

D'Avaugour, more obedient to his Sovereign than to his Bishop, returned to France as bidden. Subsequently he entered the service of the Emperor of Germany and died bravely in action defending Croatia against the Turks.

Even though the population of New France was still only two or three thousand, of which less than a thousand were in Quebec, the latter place was, by the Edict of 1663, constituted a city. In that year, one hundred families, comprising some five hundred people, came from France to settle in Quebec, their support being guaranteed by the King himself.

In spite of Royal concern, the affairs of New France were in the greatest disorder and badly required the hand of a strong, wise, determined, diplomatic leader, who could follow up the plan laid out for Government-by-Sovereign Council. Such a man the new Governor assuredly was not!

Augustin de Saffray, Chevalier de Mezy, had been chosen for the position of Governor by no less a person than Bishop Laval, and, inevitably, de Mezy had received the appointment. Laval and de Mezy had been students together in a Catholic institution and had, it seemed, similar religious views. Doubtless these things occasioned Laval's choice.

The new governor reached Quebec on September 15th, 1663, (the earthquakes had scarcely subsided), and together with the Bishop set about inaugurating the new Council. Unexpectedly, differences arose. Laval considered that his voice should be heard in matters of state and insisted on the appointment of certain gentlemen to the Council, and authorized their appointment himself. De Mezy, considering this his prerogative, promptly disapproved of the gentlemen and deposed them. Eventually he ordered their return to France. This was indeed high-handed procedure in defiance of the man who had brought about the governor's appointment. Laval was extremely annoyed, and an open breach ominously appeared between the two erstwhile friends. From this time on, they quarrelled incessantly and often over the most trivial incidents.

As the months passed and the Governor maintained his arrogant and indifferent attitude, Laval stepped lightly from the political to the clerical and excommunicated the offending Governor. This was something de Mezy had not anticipated; it was a staggering blow to a man who had always been faithful to his church.

In a letter, dated February 27th, 1664, de Mezy wrote home explaining that he had acted as he did that he "might in Canada lead a holy life in furthering the glory of God, the service of the King, and the welfare of the colony."

Meanwhile, like a never healing, ever recurrent sore on the body of infant Canada, was the scourge of the Indians, ceaseless in their efforts to wipe out the paleface, abating at times only to allow their tribes to recuperate and to replace their weapons. The intermittent expeditions of the French, allied more strongly than ever with the tribes who also lived in fear of the Iroquois, had partially cauterized the wound and brought the Iroquois to the point of hypocritically avowing themselves ready to consider peace.

De Mezy received the Indian deputation in the Council Chambers of the Château St. Louis, showed them every courtesy, listened patiently to their long harangues, and then abruptly advised them that he put so little faith in their intention to carry out their promises that he would, as and when he saw fit, carry the war into their country. These were strong words and measures indeed for a man who was harassed and upset, broken in spirit and failing in health, sustained only by the belief that he was doing his duty.

Laval had reported him to France on so many occasions that it was momentarily expected that the King would cause an investigation to be made, and de Mezy thereby hoped for justification of his actions. Before it could take place, however, he fell very ill. Suddenly his quarrel with his Bishop assumed the weight and proportion that only the unconfessed endure when refused absolution.

The Bishop, on becoming aware of the presence of death in the Château, relented so far as to have it made known to the Governor that should he wish to repent and admit the error of his ways, he would not be denied the rights of his church. And so peace was made, and de Mezy died on May 6th, 1665, after a brief rule of seventeen months. In his will he bequeathed his soul (he possessed little else for he was always a poor man) to God and the Virgin, and begged all the Saints in Heaven to intercede for him. He was buried, as he requested, in the cemetery for the poor of the Hôtel Dieu.

With the tragic end of the Chevalier de Mezy, who had scarcely had a chance to prove his worth, Quebec embarked upon a more colourful career. The Château St. Louis underwent a miraculous transformation, becoming the seat of a vice-regal court such as had never before embellished it. Gone was the monasticism of the clerics and semi-clerics; they were never again to hold sway over the government of New France, no matter what measures were taken by the Bishop. The territory was now to be governed by three men—a Lieutenant-General representing the French King in all his transatlantic possessions, a Governor who was in charge of the provinces of New France, and an Intendant whose duties required him to act as administrator of justice, treasurer of finances, and chief of police.

The broad white standard, emblazoned with the golden lilies of France, flew gaily at the masthead of the flagship as the portly and glamourous figure of Alexandre de Prouville, Marquis de Tracy, Lieutenant-General in New France, was conveyed up the sparkling St. Lawrence river, to land with all possible pageantry at the port of Quebec on a sunny day in June, 1665.

Nothing to compare with the pomp of this arrival had ever been seen in New France! All the Quebeckers, more joyously excited than they had been in many long and harrowing years, gathered at the river's edge to welcome the greatest personage who had ever come to New France. While guns boomed a royal salute from the Fort St. Louis, the brilliant procession, a lavish feast for the eyes of the poverty-stricken, a wonderful parade straight from the heart of the homeland, moved up the slope, and, to the satisfaction of Bishop Laval, who was present in all his splendid robes, went directly to the church. The bells rang a wild paean of welcome.

De Tracy, though tired from his lengthy and miserable journey, and possessed of a fever that made him appear every day of his sixty-two years, moved with the greatest dignity amid the tumult of the reception. He was led by twenty-four guards in royal livery and followed by pages and valets in brilliant attire A thousand soldiers of the Carignan-Salières regiment, as fine a body of men as could be found anywhere in the French kingdom—and gorgeous they were in their plumed helmets and embossed tunics!—brought up the rear of the regal entourage. The Marquis' personal retinue of noblemen surrounded him, their costumes only a little less splendid than his own, rich with lace and ribbons, and dashingly epauletted in gold.

Upon arrival at the church, de Tracy, by a simple act of humility, won completely the heart of the stern Bishop. Quietly, unobstrusively, he moved aside the *prie dieu* placed for him. A cushion was speedily brought to him, but this, too, he pushed aside. The King's representative in the New World knelt on the bare stone floor of the cathedral while the representative of God in the New World benignly raised his hand in blessing.

Daniel de Remi, Seigneur de Courcelles, the new Governor of New France, and Jean Talon, the Intendant, had set sail from France with the Marquis but had been delayed by storms at sea and did not arrive until September 12th of that year. Although their welcome by no means equalled the reception of the Marquis, it was nevertheless a day of rejoicing. They were accompanied by more men of the famous Carignan regiment, the very sight of their numbers bringing tears of relief to the eyes of the harassed settlers. Of these three distinguished gentlemen, Talon stands out most prominently in the eyes of posterity. He saw a future for the country beyond fur trading and farming. In this belief he promoted ship-building, established a brewery, began the growing of hemp, the art of weaving, and tanning, encouraged mining and exploration. His great interest and efforts in New France's industrial possibilities resulted in the foundation of many of Quebec's industries. The years of his sojourn in Canada were so fruitful that before his return to France he had placed the colony on a sound economic basis for the first time in its history. And so faithfully did he carry out the instructions given him by Colbert, the King's wise Foreign Minister, that he subsequently became known as the "Colbert of Canada".

De Courcelles' service to Canada was chiefly the well-nigh impossible task of quelling the Iroquois. He made sundry sorties against them but was most unlucky in these attempts. Upon one such occasion he had planned a particularly large and ambitious expedition to be carried out by the Carignan-Salières allied with the Algonquins. It failed disastrously because the Algonquins did not come forward with the promised assistance, and the new troops found themselves as yet unequal to the diversities of Indian warfare. For this perfidy on the part of the Algonquins, de Courcelles blamed the Jesuits who, it seemed, had complete control over their Algonquin converts and did not, at that time, approve of making war on the Iroquois. As a result of this, there arose considerable ill-feeling between Church and State in Quebec—the old trouble that took so little reviving.

History recalls, too, with a touch of whimsy, the embarrassing attempt made by de Courcelles to rout a tribe located in the Lake Champlain district. He lost his bearings and ended up somewhere in Dutch territory (where now stands the city of Schenectady), and to add to his chagrin, he was there quickly informed that the area was in English hands.

The Marquis' role was one of general overseer and mediator in the differences between the clergy and the body politic, and one of his foremost duties was the establishment of the Civil Government. His role as mediator was doubtless a full-time job, and for two years the Marquis endured with admirable fortitude and wisdom the constant differences and bickering. During that time his disposition grew ever more testy due, in large part, to his constant misery from gout. In 1667, he and his magnificent entourage departed for France, taking much of the splendour and glamour that had brought a breath of Fontainebleau and Versailles to the homesick colonists and to the old Château St. Louis. Three years later de Tracy died at Bordeaux.

Talon and de Courcelles remained in New France until 1672. The former, the hardiest of the three men, suffered no particular defects from his service, but de Courcelles' health had broken and he was urged to return home. Needless to say, they left a regretful colony behind them. Both died in Paris, Talon in 1694 and de Courcelles in 1698.

Little has been told here of the great Talon, for it is not the purpose of this narrative to record the biographies of great men except in so far as they affected, or were affected by, the great grey castle on the cliff. Evidences of the foresight and ingenuity of this benefactor of the pioneers may be found in Quebec today, and they form a greater monument to him than does the effigy of his person which now graces the outer wall of the Legislative Building in the city of Quebec.

During the period 1665 to 1670, the "King's girls" arrived in New France. The cold-blooded commercial angle of this transaction in human life leaves the modern reader of these old letters with no slight sensation of amazement. Cargoes of young women were shipped from France to Quebec, and, within a fortnight of their landing on this continent, they were married to men whom they had never before seen. However, though each was allowed to pick a husband from the group of waiting bachelors, there was no dilly-dallying, languishing, or capriciousness. Though many of the girls came from charitable institutions of various kinds, their conduct had to be exemplary, and they were treated with respect and consideration. After all, were they not rendering a patriotic service to their King and country?

The official correspondence on this colonizing venture is unique. One is intrigued with such excerpts[4] as,

Colbert to Talon, 15th May, 1669: "The King sends 150 girls to be married, 6 companies of 50 men, 30 officers or gentlemen, 200 other persons."

Colbert to de Courcelles, 19th April, 1670: "Encourage early marriage, so that by the multiplication of children the colony may have the means of increase."

Talon to the King, 10th September, 1670: "165 girls arrived, 30 remain unmarried, 150 to 200 more asked for."

Talon to the King, 10th November, 1670: "The girls sent last year are married, and almost all pregnant or mothers."

Talon to Colbert, 2nd November, 1671: "Between 600 and 700 children born, inexpedient to send out girls next year."

A humorous account of this barter is given us by Francis Park-

[4]Dr. William Kingsford's *History of Canada, Vol. I,* Footnote, page 359.

man, that most faithful of historians, of whose valuable labours no student of Canadian history dares deny himself. "At the end of a fortnight not one was left. I am told that the plumpest were taken first, because it was thought that, being less active, they were more likely to keep at home, and that they could resist the winter cold better. Those who wanted a wife applied to the directresses, to whom they were obliged to make known their possessions and means of livelihood before taking from one of the three classes the girl whom they found most to their liking. The marriage was concluded forthwith, with the help of a priest and a notary, and the next day the governor-general caused the couple to be presented with an ox, a cow, a pair of swine, a pair of fowls, two barrels of salted meat, and eleven crowns in money."[5] In due time there were rewards for the number of offspring resulting from such marriages.

A glance at Quebec's lighter side during that period reveals that on the night of February 4th 1667[6], before the Marquis de Tracy returned to France, the first ball held in New France took place in a mansion belonging at that time to Judge L. Théantre Chartier de Lotbinière, then Lieutenant-General of the French King. It is said that this building was on Mount Carmel street, which today borders the Château Frontenac. Various historians have suggested that the ball was held in the Château St. Louis. It was a brilliant affair, with all the available men (including the officers of the Carignan Regiment) wearing all the available masculine finery that a quasi-regal court could provide. And the ladies—(oh, bliss! there were now nearly enough to go around!)—were enchanting in ball gowns that outshone anything New France had yet known; and it mattered not at all that the styles were hopelessly outdated compared to those of the court circle at Versailles which would have scorned to be seen in such outmoded apparel. The evening was gay with music and dancing, good wines and delicacies, and was climaxed by the grand entrance of the Marquis, which was worthy of the King himself at a court function. Military music throbbed through the old castle and mingled with the vivacious laughter of the sons and daughters of old France.

[5]Mr. Parkman is here quoting from the Baron de la Hontan's *Nouveaux Voyages,* Vol. I, (1709).

[6]J. M. Le Moine in *Quebec, Past and Present.*

Chapter Four

SYNONYMOUS WITH New France is the name of one of her greatest men: the Comte de Frontenac. His name evokes a picture of a debonair gentleman with serious eyes, doffing a wide-brimmed plumed hat, tossing his exquisite cape over his shoulder, placing his hand defiantly on the hilt of his sword, stepping forward crisply in high leather boots.

The imprint of this man's appearance on the Canadian scene is ineradicable. The history of this dominion cannot be read without reading of the Comte de Frontenac and his activities. He is remembered today as the man who defied Phipps, as the man who built the first walls about Quebec, and after whom the Château Frontenac is named. Though the Comte did not build this namesake—that was left to men of equal vision who were to come later—the Château Frontenac is *un palais* that proudly perpetuates his memory and of which he would be immensely proud could he see it as it is today.

Upon his arrival in Quebec in September, 1672, the Comte de Frontenac found the Château St. Louis in need of restoration. It seemed as if it were waiting for the strong hand, the extravagant taste, the flair for the magnificent that was Frontenac. The work done upon it by the Marquis de Tracy, in his effort to make it a suitable place for a Lieutenant-General, had not been finished. Certain sections had scarcely been touched since the earthquake of 1663. It now became evident that the foundations had been not a little displaced at that time; cracks were appearing in the walls and ceilings causing considerable uneasiness.

Though the Comte was deeply impressed with the beauty of Quebec and the surrounding country, he was far from pleased with this château that was to be his home. Concurrently with writing words of praise for New France to Colonial Minister Colbert, he wrote asking for money to spend in repairing the Château St. Louis. Shortly after his arrival he wrote, under date of November 2nd, 1672, "Nothing appears to me so fair or so superb as the position of this town of Quebec. It could not be better located as the future capital of a great empire."[1] In 1681, nine years later, he wrote, "The walls (of the château) are all down. There are neither gates nor guardhouse; the whole place is open." Then, in a letter of thanks to the King for a little money to spend on the old building, he stated that, "I shall erect a new building," (an extravagant statement, since the money was quite insufficient) "trying meanwhile to avoid being buried under the old one which is what I expect each time the wind blows hard." Ten years later, 1691, still pleading the same cause, he importuned the King for twenty thousand francs for repairs, principally, he explained, to re-roof the building with slate. There seems to have been little consideration given to his requests for, in 1692, he wrote to say that the ruin had reached such a stage that he was compelled to have the workmen labour all night to prevent its collapse.

Volumes have been written on the character and career of this illustrious personage. Some say he was high-handed, rash, proud, temperamental, only slightly religious; that he was cruel, obstinate, dominant, imperious. Others dwell upon his statesmanship, skill, sagacity, dignity, oratory, courage, courtesy, determination, and the faithfulness with which he guarded the trust placed in him. And yet—all these things were the Comte de Frontenac!

The rebuilding of the Château St. Louis was but a minor detail in the career of Frontenac as Governor and Lieutenant-General in New France. His title, in itself, was imposing and weighty:

> "Louis de Buade, Comte de Palluau et Frontenac, Seigneur de l'Isle Savary, Mestre de Camp du Regiment de Normandie, Marechal de Camp dans (les) Armées du Roi, et Gouverneur et Lieutenant-Général en Canada, Acadie, Isle Terreneuve et autre pays de la France septentrionale."

In the discharge of all the duties which his lengthy title entailed, never once can Frontenac be accused of proving inadequate. He had unbounded faith in New France; he was convinced of her immense possibilities; and from the beginning he endeavoured to prove his faith and to realize those nebulous possibilities.

Like all powerful men, Frontenac was the object of criticism

[1]Ernest Gagnon in *Le Fort et Château St. Louis.*

from those less powerful, and from his enemies of whom he managed to collect a surprising number. The Intendant Duchesneau was jealous of him, and throughout their sojourn together in New France the Intendant aped the man who was his superior and assumed, quite wrongfully, whenever he dared, many of the powers that belonged only to the Governor. With a man of Frontenac's temperament, this was a situation likely to cause trouble. The position of Intendant had been originated to act as a check on the activities of the King's representative in New France; and in the fulfilment of his duties, Duchesneau took care to exercise to the limit, if not to exaggerate, the powers invested in him. Naturally, the Comte was called upon to put the man in his place, and this resulted in quarrels. Of the two men, Duchesneau was the more religious. He was a close friend of Bishop Laval, with whom he saw eye to eye in most matters; therefore, they supported each other to their mutual benefit. As a consequence, the Bishop and the Governor could rarely agree upon anything. Thus began anew the old internal troubles of the colony, and they did not abate until Bishop Laval was replaced by Bishop St. Vallier in 1688.

Never before had a Governor of New France stepped down from his pedestal to the extent of meeting the savages on their own ground, eating with them, dancing war dances with them, smoking their long white pipes, and generally fraternizing with them. New France was amazed but accorded him a grudging admiration; the Indians accorded him a respect that was tinged with awe. He learned their language and his oratory excelled their own—and they listened to him. He gradually brought the savages to the realization that the power wielded by the land across the great water was not to be defied without disastrous consequences.

Frontenac was master of the Indian situation during his entire stay in New France, no matter what methods the tribes took to harass him and his little colony on the cliff, or the few forts that were now strung out as far west as the great lakes. Those tribes who could neither antagonize him nor ally themselves with him, betook themselves and their trade southward to befriend, and to be befriended by, the English. This caused a situation which, fraught with dangerous implication for the future as it was, gave Frontenac no little concern. The southern colonies were making no secret of their designs on certain of New France's westerly forts, and should their armies become allied with the Indians, the strength of the English would be formidable.

Possessed of much military wisdom and training, Frontenac was well aware that he who would conquer New France must capture Quebec—first or last. So he began to fortify it as it had never before been fortified. With a zest that only the most determined and most confident know, he undertook to build a wall around the settlement. It consisted of pickets, ten feet in height, walled up on the inner side with earth and stone. At vantage points eleven stone bastions and redoubts were mounted with guns. The wall went westward from the Château, midway between Mount Carmel and St. Louis streets, over what is now known as Haldimand Hill, westward again to St. Ursule street, thence northwestward, northerly through the intersection of Ste. Angele and Ste. Anne streets to St. Stanislas street, ending somewhere in the vicinity of the present Palace Hill.

In 1682 Frontenac was recalled by the King, the result, no doubt, of the endless unfavourable reports sent to France by the Intendant Duchesneau, Bishop Laval, and various others whom he had made his enemies in one way or another. The Comte was in his seventieth year when King Louis sent him back to Canada seven years later in the hope that he would restore the order that had slipped so badly in the interim under the two governors, Denonville and La Barre.

The colony of Quebec welcomed Frontenac with a warm celebration, a sort of homecoming; a cannonade from the guns of the fort announced to all New France that the leader had returned; there were long harangues from civil and church dignitaries, some of whom had been the means of his recall; the evening was festive with a torchlight parade and fireworks.

Frontenac's first charge, after restoring order in New France, was to conquer New York in an effort to prevent English-Dutch expansion. Failing outright conquest, he intended to hem them in by colonizing the banks of the newly-discovered Mississippi and gradually force them toward the Atlantic seaboard. After a review of the garrisons of Quebec, Montreal and Three Rivers, Frontenac found them fewer in number than anticipated and far from well-disciplined. Allied with Indians he managed eventually to form three war parties of picked men, one from each of the three towns; the first was to strike at Albany (it was subsequently deviated to Schenectady); the second to strike at the settlements of New Hampshire; and the third at the settlements of Maine. Noble and courageous men, whose names are a part of history, led the troops: D'Ailleboust de Mantet, Le Moyne de Saint-Hélène, Le Moyne d'Iberville, Le Moyne de Bienville, Repentigny de Montesson, and Le Ber du Chesne. . . .

Schenectady was taken with disgraceful slaughter of the innocent, and the dwellings were reduced to ashes; so were many settlements in New Hampshire and Maine. The war ordered by the King of France on the heretics of North America, the most peaceful of all his enemies, was most successful.

Little wonder the Comte de Frontenac expected an attack from the south sooner or later. In those days England and France were enemies and required small cause for an exchange of blows on one side of the Atlantic or the other. European affairs were in a particularly waspish condition. James the Second of England, a friend of the French King, had been deposed—and justly so—by his own people. In his stead William of Orange had been set up as King, an enemy of France—a Protestant.

The governors of the English provinces in North America, realizing they were in imminent danger of being surrounded if not wiped out by the French to the north, put their heads together and laid careful plans for the downfall of New France. Their armies were to go overland towards Montreal under General Winthrop and their ships were to go *via* the St. Lawrence under Admiral Sir William Phipps, to converge finally upon Quebec.

Charlevoix, the historian, tells of an interesting sidelight to these plans — though he does not guarantee the truth of the story. The English formed a scheme that certain boxes of contaminated clothing, carrying smallpox infection, would go ahead of their overland army, ostensibly for their use in the campaign, but which would be placed where they might readily be stolen by the

French. The boxes chanced to fall instead into the hands of the savages who were scheduled to join Winthrop at a prearranged point. The childlike curiosity of the savages led them to open the boxes and to masquerade in the clothing they contained. Soon the Indians fell ill with smallpox and many died. Charlevoix adds that the weak friendship then existing between Indian and Englishman was not strengthened by this misfortune. Thus, the ill-assorted allies fell out among themselves at a crucial hour when England most needed their combined strength.

So much for Winthrop's effort overland.

On the morning of October 16th, 1690, the sun rose over the hills of Quebec and found the English fleet in the basin below the city, serenely riding at anchor.

Frontenac, from a vantage point in the Château St. Louis, which gave him a commanding view of the whole river, watched and waited, while every man of his garrison and his colony stood to arms and every woman and child took refuge behind the walls. They had not long to wait. Soon a boat put out from the admiral's ship and landed in the cul-de-sac below the cliff. Frontenac's officers met the envoy it carried. The envoy, probably chosen because of his knowledge of the French language, was led, blindfold, to the Château St. Louis, *via* the most tortuous way of ascent. The inhabitants and the soldiers mingled and talked much, rattled musketry, in an endeavour to create the impression to the blindfolded Englishman that their numbers were many and well armed. It is said that the crowd taunted him with cries of "*Colin Maillard*".[2] Frontenac awaited him in the great reception hall. The bandage about the Englishman's eyes was removed, allowing him to witness the brilliant spectacle that had been especially prepared for him—though he was not supposed to get that impression.

The Governor was his most gorgeous self. Even his broad-brimmed hat with its rich ostrich plume lay on a table near him for added effect. At his left hip swung the rapier that seemed almost a part of him. By his side stood the Bishop and the Intendant, each in the full dress of his office. Around them stood the officers and men of the Governor's staff, resplendent in their finest

[2]'Blind Man's Buff'.

uniforms and carefully-curled perukes. It is related that, although as surprised as his enemies hoped he would be, the Englishman conducted himself with befitting dignity, and, with a flourish worthy of Frontenac himself, unrolled the imposing parchment he carried and read in clipped accents the message from his Commander, Sir William Phipps:

> "To Count Frontenac, Lieutenant-General and Governor for the French king at Canada; or in his absence, to his Deputy, or him of them in chief command at Quebeck:
>
> "The war between the crowns of England and France doth not only sufficiently warrant, but the destruction made by the French and Indians, under your command and encouragement, upon the persons and estates of their Majesties' subjects of New England, without provocation on their part, hath put them under the necessity of this expedition for their own security and satisfaction. And although the cruelties and barbarities used against them by the French and Indians might, upon the present opportunity, prompt unto a severe revenge, yet, being desirous to avoid all unhumane and unchristian-like actions, and to prevent the shedding of blood as much as may be,
>
> "I, William Phipps, Knight, do hereby, in the name and in the behalf of their most excellent Majesties, William and Mary, King and Queen of England, Scotland, France and Ireland, Defenders of the Faith, and by order of their said Majesties' government of the Massachusetts-colony in New England, demand a present surrender of your forts and castles undemolished, and the things and other stores, unimbezzled, with a seasonable delivery of all captives; together with a surrender of all your persons and estates to my dispose: Upon the doing whereof, you may expect mercy from me, as a Christian, according to what shall be found for their Majesties' service and the subjects' security. Which, if you refuse forthwith to do, I am come provided, and am resolved, by the help of God, in whom I trust, by force of arms to revenge all wrongs and injuries offered, and bring you under subjection to the Crown of England, and, when too late, make you wish you had accepted of the favour tendered.
>
> "Your answer positive in an hour," (continued the envoy with the flourish of a timepiece) "returned by your own trum-

pet, with the return of mine, is required upon the peril that will ensue."[3]

As soon as the document had been read in English it was translated into French.

This was indeed a gauntlet thrown at the proud Frontenac—and not at his feet but in his face! It takes little imagination to realize the hot anger that inflamed the fighting governor at such a summons so confident of his surrender. His reply was immediate. His voice rang icily stern in the great hall of the old Château:

> "I will not keep you waiting so long. Tell your general that I do not recognize King William; and that the Prince of Orange, who so styles himself, is a usurper, who has violated the most sacred laws of blood in attempting to dethrone his father-in-law. I know no king of England but King James. Your general ought not to be surprised at the hostilities which he says that the French have carried on in the colony of Massachusetts; for, as the king my master has taken the king of England under his protection, and is about to replace him on his throne by force of arms, he might have expected that His Majesty would order me to make war on a people who have rebelled against their lawful prince.
>
> "Even if your general had offered me conditions a little more gracious, and if I had a mind to accept them, does he suppose that these brave gentlemen would give their consent, and advise me to trust a man who broke his agreement with the governor of Port Royal, or a rebel who has failed in his duty to his king, and forgotten all the favours he had received from him, to follow a prince who pretends to be the liberator of England and the defender of the faith, and yet destroys the laws and privileges of the kingdom and overthrows its religion? The divine justice which your general invokes in his letter will not fail to punish such acts severely."[4]

When the envoy demanded that these words be written for conveyance to his commander, the Count's voice was contemptuous as he answered with the defiant words that have echoed down the years even as they then echoed in the old Castle: "I will answer

[3]From Francis Parkman's *Count Frontenac and New France under Louis XIV.* (Little, Brown & Co., Boston, 1887).

[4]Francis Parkman in *Count Frontenac and New France under Louis XIV.* Other texts differ slightly in wording though not in purport.

your general only by the mouths of my cannon, that he may learn that a man like me is not to be summoned after this fashion. Let him do his best, and I will do mine."[5]

Scarcely had the emissary reboarded the admiral's ship than the guns of the Fort St. Louis gave out their first salvos of defiance. Almost instantly Phipps replied in kind. And yet, in spite of the high-sounding words exchanged, the siege was no more than an exchange of gunfire. Phipps made no determined assault upon the city. He bombarded it sporadically for two days with guns too light in weight to have much effect, whereas his ships suffered much damage from the guns of the fort. The small land force which had gained a precarious footing on the opposite bank of the St. Charles river became bogged down in the mud. Sickness overtook many of the invaders; others were picked off by French and Indian snipers. A week passed before Phipps lost heart, weighed anchor, and slipped out with the tide on the evening of October 21st.

Phipps was a self-made man. One cannot but admire him—even though he did insult the good Comte de Frontenac and bombard the city of Quebec. After all, he did no more than Wolfe did some sixty-nine years later. Born of humble parentage, on the banks of the Kennebec river, of a family of twenty-six children (all of the same mother), he spent his youth as a sheepherder. At the age of eighteen he went to Boston, became a ship's carpenter, and also learned how to read and write. Like many boys he dreamed of sailing the Spanish Main and discovering sunken galleons laden with treasure—but few boys have their dreams come true as Phipps eventually did. He managed to interest certain wealthy persons in his ideas, and through them procured a ship; he roved the seas for many years before he found exactly what he sought: gold, silver, jewels, valued at £300,000 sterling, of which his share was £16,000. To add to his glory, he received a baronetcy. After his unsuccessful siege of Quebec, Sir William was made a Governor of Massachusetts, but was later recalled for assaulting with his cane a Captain of the Royal Navy who was a Collector of Customs for the port of Boston.[6] He died in 1693.

[5]Francis Parkman, *Op. cit.*

[6]The Reverend William H. Withrow in *A Popular History of the Dominion of Canada,* (1878).

Quebec's rejoicing at her deliverance from Phipps was short-lived. A familiar enemy from within now stalked across the city. Hunger. Famine, such as would have permitted Phipps to win the siege had he delayed a little longer, now stretched with quiet horror over the colony. And it was almost winter. . . .

In his book, *The Old Régime in Canada,* (1887), Francis Parkman tells us that a tablet bearing a Latin inscription was found by workmen in 1854 in a garden adjoining the Château St. Louis, while they were in the process of lengthening the Terrace. The newspaper, *The Quebec Mercury*, in its issue of September 2nd, 1854, gives this account of the discovery:

> Most Interesting Discovery
>
> "The extension of Durham Terrace brought to light the cornerstone of the first French fortifications erected at this place. The inscription on a plate of copper informs us that it was laid in 1693 by Louis de Baude, Comte de Frontenac, 2nd Governor of la Nouvelle France, during the reign of Louis XIV."

Le Journal de Québec of September 2nd, 1854, gives the wording of this plaque which, translated, is as follows:

> "In the year of redemption, 1693, under the reign of the Most August, Most Invincible, and Most Christian King of France, Louis the Great, fourteenth of that name, the most excellent Louis de Buade, Comte of Frontenac, Governor for the second time of all New France, seeing that the rebellious inhabitants of New England, who three years ago were repulsed, routed and completely vanquished by him, when they besieged this town of Quebec, are threatening to renew the siege this very year, has caused to be built, at the expense of the King, this Citadel, with the fortifications adjoining thereto, for the defence of the country, for the security of the people, and for confounding yet again that nation perfidious alike towards its God and its lawful King, and he (Frontenac) has placed here this first stone."

What became of this plaque? Very little seems to be known of its whereabouts. It occupies no prominent place on or in any of the public buildings of Quebec where one might expect to find it.

Mr. P. G. Roy advises that he is "under the impression that

this plaque was kept in the Chasseur Museum" and that this museum "started by Mr. Chasseur, was later transferred to the Parliament Building which was, at that time, situated on top of Mountain Hill, where is now Montmorency-Laval Park".[7] The Parliament Building to which Mr. Roy refers was rebuilt after a fire on February 1st, 1854, and was burned again in 1883. If the Chasseur Museum was in the building at that time, it is highly possible that the plaque was lost with all the treasures of art, literature and mineralogy that were destroyed, and that what remained of it was removed with the rest of the debris.

And yet. . . in a charming little book called *A Quebec Sketch Book*, written by Esther Brann in 1929, there is mention of a cornerstone of the Citadel bearing similar wording, and date, as on Frontenac's plaque. If this is the same plaque, where is it now?

Comte Frontenac was never satisfied with the grandeur he managed to display in and about his château. Gradually he created a little court of Versailles in this outpost on the edge of civilization, and the ceremonies conducted within it were in all respects worthy of the parent court. Magnificent balls were held—(scarcely in keeping with the hunger of the populace)—when the Château St. Louis was thronged with lovely ladies in rich gowns and jewels, with tall powdered headresses and fluttering fans; the highest officers of the garrison and of the Governor's entourage were equally as gorgeous in their exaggerated wigs and velvet costumes, paying elaborate court to the beauties about them.

Of course the clergy frowned in dark disapproval at these gatherings, but still the gaiety went on. To add yet more to their disapproval, the little theatricals that were arranged in the great hall of the Château portrayed some of the more wicked plays, and when Molière's *Tartuffe* was to be enacted, the good Bishop St. Vallier, using every means at his command, finally compelled Frontenac to cancel it. Invitations to the dinners, suppers, and balls at the Governor's palace were avidly sought after and well worth scheming to obtain. It is, and was then, a cause for regret that Madame la Comtesse did not grace the social régime of Quebec with her charming presence and famous wit.

[7]In a letter to the author, Mr. Roy so advised his thoughts on this plaque.

Perhaps here, then, is the moment to pry a little into the personal life of this handsome nobleman whose beautiful wife refused to live with him in Quebec. Their love affair was, we are told, as romantic in its early days as any romance could be. She was the lovely Anne de la Grange-Trianon, daughter of the Sieur de Neuville. Because of her father's opposition to the match, Anne eloped with the Comte when she was but sixteen years old. They were married in October, 1648, at the little church of St. Pierre aux Boeufs which was the "Gretna Green" of France in those days. They were happy enough for a few years, and a son was born to them, but the high court circle in which they moved, with all its outrageous extravagance, soon exhausted their not-extensive fortunes. As is often the case under such circumstances, tempers grew short, and before long the handsome pair could scarcely endure each other.

The Fronde rebellion, directed against rule by Mazarin while King Louis XIV was still a minor, was fanatically supported by certain ladies of the court, among them a close friend of the Comtesse de Frontenac, a cousin of the young King, Mademoiselle de Montpensier. The Comtesse joined her friend, earned a warlike reputation for herself, and dropped her husband into the background of her life. In her memoirs, Mademoiselle de Montpensier writes of a visit made by the Comte to his Comtesse while at St. Fargeau—some two or three days journey from Paris in the era of carriages. "Instead of going to talk with her husband," writes Mademoiselle de Montpensier, "she went and hid herself, crying and screaming because he had said that he would like to have her company that evening. I was very much astonished, especially as I had never before perceived her aversion to him."[8] Mademoiselle then goes on to say that remonstrances with the young Comtesse were futile, that she became hysterical, and that only the curé with his holy water to exorcise her proved successful in quieting her.

So it is understandable that, when Frontenac accepted the appointment as the King's representative in New France, the Comtesse would not consider accompanying him, a matter which, it is said, gave the Comte so little concern as to be highly unflattering

[8]Francis Parkman, *Count Frontenac and New France under Louis XIV.*

to the lady. To her credit be it said, nevertheless, that, upon all occasions, she gave her absent husband the full weight of her influence in the French court, which was by no means insignificant. The historian, Saint Simon, has left a record of her later years which tells us that she died at the age of seventy-five, still lovely, still gay, her apartment the centre of the élite of French society.

For many years there hung in the Versailles Gallery the picture of an attractive woman in the battle dress of the goddess Minerva. It is the Comtesse de Frontenac in her costume indicative of her Fronde activities. In a corner of the canvas may be observed the words, "Anne de la Grange-Trianon". It is a plump figure, full and round of face, voluptuous mouth, straight and somewhat overlong nose, and high forehead. Her hair is hidden by the gilded helmet which she wears, atop which six long plumes float; her shoulders slope gracefully; on her right shoulder is slung a quiver of arrows; on her left arm she carries a shield; in her right hand a bow. If one is not able to visit the Versailles gallery in a search for this painting, a rather good reproduction of it can be seen in the Château Frontenac where it hangs at present on the same wall as an almost equally good one of her illustrious husband.

****

It is three o'clock in the afternoon of November 28th, 1698. All Quebec is waiting for news of its aged and ailing Governor, the indomitable Frontenac. That he is dying, everyone knows and grieves. Very quietly and peacefully he ends a career that has been neither quiet nor peaceful. He has made his peace with Laval who has absolved him of all his offences. And all New France weeps. Never has there been such universal grief in the country. Drapes of gloomy hue are hung about the portals of the Château St. Louis which had been so gay while the Governor lived; even the flag on the main tower droops forlornly in the chill, wet November air.

A month after the death of the Comte, the Intendant Champigny duly reported his demise to the Colonial Office in France. "On the 28th of last month," wrote the Intendant, "Monsieur le Comte de Frontenac died, with the sentiments of a true Christian. After all our disputes, you will hardly believe, Monseigneur, how truly and deeply I am touched by his death. He treated me during his illness in a manner so obliging that I should be utterly devoid of gratitude if I did not feel thankful to him."

It was left to the incomparable rambling chronicler, Charlevoix, to sum up some years later all that Canada's first real statesman had meant to her. "After all, New France owed to him all that she was at the time of his death, and the people soon perceived the great void he had left behind him."

In his will, the Comte de Frontenac made provision for Mass to be said daily on his behalf for one year, and thereafter upon the anniversary of his death, in which his wife was to share upon her demise. He left all that he possessed to his wife with a last strange request: that his heart be encased in a silver casket and sent to her.[9] What prompted this enigmatic gesture towards one who had cared so little for him? Was it, perhaps, the desire of a lonely old man to have some part of himself return to rest among his forefathers and not to rest forgotten in a savage country? Cruel gossip tells us—and may those who repeat it for truth be forgiven (unless they have more proof of its veracity than now exists)—that the Comtesse promptly sent it back to New France with the message that in life it had not belonged to her, therefore she did not want it in death. Mr. Ernest Myrand in his book, *Frontenac et Ses Amis,* (1902) says that this legend is "une anecdote scandaleuse . . . pas d'origine française, mais canadienne, québecquoise seulement . . ." Nevertheless, when the Count's remains were removed from the Church of the Recollets some years later because of a fire, and placed in the Basilica of Quebec where they rest in peace, a small silver casket was found on his coffin.[10]

****

It is regrettable that our story cannot proceed without recourse to that period of seven years between Frontenac's terms as Governor, during which two weak and fumbling creatures assumed, successively, the post recently filled so capably.

[9]Dr. William Kingsford, *History of Canada,* Vol. II.

[10]"Il parait, d'après M. le Major Lafleur et M. de Gaspé (auteur des Anciens Canadiens) lequel fut témoin oculaire de l'incendie de l'église des Recollets, que les cercueils de plomb qui se trouvaient sous les voûtes de l'église, placés sur des tablettes en fer, étaient en partie fondus. La petite boîte de plomb contenant le coeur de M. de Frontenac, se trouvait, dit-on, sur son cercueil."—Msgr. Tanquay in *Dictionnaire Génealogique,* as quoted by Myrand.

Le Febvre de la Barre arrived with his Intendant, des Meules, on August 4th, 1682, to find the Lower Town of Quebec in ruins and ashes from a devastating fire which had swept it just prior to his arrival. An inauspicious reception indeed! Before he withdrew to France, Frontenac had done his utmost to acquaint La Barre with existing conditions and to advise him of the best possible procedure. Since the new Governor had been given orders to attack the Iroquois, if he deemed it necessary, with the stipulation that he should first make very certain that he would be successful, La Barre laid bold plans to carry out an attack. He wrote to France for a thousand or so soldiers. The King promptly advised him that he did not find it convenient to send more troops at this time.

Having been a soldier for the greater part of his life, La Barre, now sixty years of age, was vainly, almost ridiculously, proud of his military record; he insisted upon being addressed as *Monsieur le Général* instead of *Monsieur le Gouverneur*.

On May 30th, 1683, La Barre again wrote his King for troops (having accomplished little since his first letter), saying bravely, "I will perish at their head or destroy your enemies," but when war actually was upon him he became nervous and apprehensive, deciding that he must have more assistance. "Recall me if you will not help me," he wrote the King, "for I cannot bear to see the country perish in my hands." Meanwhile, des Meules had become disgusted with *Monsieur le Général* and wrote to the Foreign Minister, "La Barre's excuses are a mere pretense—everybody is astonished and disgusted with him."

When the King did recall La Barre, he was kind about it: "Having been informed that your years do not permit you to support the fatigues inseparable with your office of governor and lieutenant-general in Canada, I send you this letter to acquaint you that I have selected M. de Denonville to serve in your place, and my intention is that, on his arrival, after resigning to him the command, with all instructions concerning it, you embark for your return to France." It was painfully obvious that the recall came none too soon for La Barre had all but undone what Frontenac had accomplished in his first term of office, in so far as the intimidation of the Indians was concerned.

Alas! the Marquis de Denonville was another of those pious soldiers who, because he wished to be both pious and a soldier, was sadly lacking in those other qualities that Canada demanded in her early years. Jacques-René de Brisay, the Marquis de Denonville, arrived in Quebec to assume the governorship of New France in August, 1685, and was accompanied by his wife and children. The voyage had been a most miserable one; crew and passengers had been alike attacked by scurvy and some of them had died on the way. Little wonder the voyage was spent, as Bishop St. Vallier said, "in prayer and the reading of the Psalms of David".

Denonville's opinion of the English to the south was one of doubt and suspicion. He believed them to be the instigators of the frequent outrages perpetrated by the Iroquois on the French. He wanted desperately to strike a blow at both Englishman and Indian in order to restore French prestige that had suffered badly under de la Barre. It is unfortunate—and hardly worth recording—that this God-fearing gentleman was weak in all his endeavours. Had he attempted less and been more successful, his name would be better remembered in the annals of New France. As it is, he is recalled more often as "one of the governors who came between Frontenac's terms".

For one thing only can we, who are interested chiefly in one historic building of the time, be grateful to the Marquis de Denonville. Without authority or money from home, he managed to build a powder magazine within the enclosure of the Fort St. Louis, with stone walls uncommonly thick even for that period, and a funnel-shaped roof. This building later was an important asset to Frontenac's "new" building, as it was eventually included in the château proper. The walls of this magazine are, to this day, a part of the rear wall of the Château Frontenac.

After his return to France we find Denonville, with no loss whatsoever of personal prestige, spending the remainder of his life in the enviable and genteel position of governor and tutor to the royal sons of France. He died on September 24th, 1710 at the age of seventy-two.

As for New France's conditions in 1689—only the second term of the Comte de Frontenac could restore them to order.

Chapter Five

FOR A WORD PICTURE of the Château St. Louis at the time of, and shortly after, the death of the Comte de Frontenac, we are indebted to Francis Parkman who gives us the following description in his book, *The Old Régime in Canada*: "The new château was not finished before 1700, and even then it had no cistern. In a pen-sketch of Quebec on a manuscript map of 1699, preserved in the Dépôt des Cartes de la Marine, the new château is distinctly represented. In front is a gallery or balcony, resting on a wall and buttresses at the edge of the cliff. Above the gallery is a range of high windows and a mansard roof. In the middle is a porch opening on the gallery; and on the left extends a battery on the ground now occupied by a garden along the brink of the cliff."[1]

The manuscript map[2] to which Mr. Parkman refers is doubtless that which has been reproduced for us in the A. L. Pinart Atlas, *Receuil de Cartes, Plans et Vues Relatifs aux Etats-Unis et au Canada—1651-1731—sous la direction de A. L. Pinart.* This is a view of Quebec in an ornamented design, at the bottom of which the natives are depicted as preparing and eating their food around a large cauldron which is suspended over a blazing wood fire. The map is titled, "Part of North America, comprising New France, New England, New Albany and New York, Pennsylvania, Virginia, Carolina, Florida, Louisiana, etc., by Jean Baptiste Louis Franquelin, King's Geographer, 1699". It forms part of the library of the Dépôt de la Marine, its number being B.4044-12. On this map, the building (*B. Le Fort*) fits the verbal description given by Mr. Parkman. Also, to the left of the Château St. Louis, is seen the Powder Magazine (C. *Magazin des Poudres*) which the Marquis de Denonville had built "without authority or money from home".

La Potherie, one of the early French-Canadian historians, who visited Quebec in 1698, has left us a word picture of the Château St. Louis which he represents as being two stories in

[1]Francis Parkman, *The Old Régime in Canada* (1887). App. F. p. 421.
[2]Plate No. 11 in the *Pinart Atlas* (Public Archives of Canada).

height.[3] The passage in his work which refers to the Château is translated by the painstaking Alfred Hawkins in his book, *Picture of Quebec*: "It stands upon the brink of a vast cliff one hundred and eighty feet high. Its fortifications are irregular having two bastions on the city side, without any ditch. The house of the Governor General is one hundred and twenty feet long, in front of which is a terrace of eighty feet, which overlooks the Lower Town and the channel. The edifice is pleasing, both as regards its interior and exterior, on account of the wings which form the building in front and rear. It is two stories high, and there is still wanting a wing of thirty-three feet long. On the side of the house there is a battery of twenty-two embrasures, partly inclosed in the building, and part without, commanding the Lower Town and the River. At four hundred paces above is Cape Diamond, four hundred and eighty feet high, upon which stands a redoubt which commands the Upper Town and the adjacent country."

Mr. P. G. Roy gives a description of the site as it was in 1709, giving as his source "Relation par lettres de l'Amérique Septentrionale, Attribuée au Pére Antoine Silvy": "One goes from the Lower Town to the Upper by a very steep and bad hill. On the height of the rock the Château St. Louis is seen, which serves as a dwelling for the governor, by the side of which there are two batteries, each provided with several cannon which are directed towards the harbour."[4]

Whether the Château St. Louis actually had two stories at this time or later, or whether one historian counted the ground floor (the floor below the level of the embankment) as one storey, and another historian did not, the fact remains that it was certainly the most impressive building in New France.

There were now three men who felt themselves quite capable of filling the boots of the deceased Governor: M. Louis Hector de Callières-Bonnevue, the Governor of Montreal; M. Jean Bochard de Champigny, the Intendant; and Philippe François Rigaud,

[3]*Histoire de l'Amérique Septentrionale depuis 1534 jusqu'à 1701* by Claude Bacqueville de le Roy de la Potherie.

[4]"On monte de la basse ville à la haute per une côte très raide et très mauvaise. On voit sur le haut du rocher le château Saint-Louis qui sert de logement au gouverneur, à côté duquel il y a deux batteries garnies chacune de plusieurs canons qui battent toutes deux sur la rade." *La Ville de Québec Sous le Régime Français.*

Marquis de Vaudreuil. It developed that he who could obtain the strongest influence would get the position.

De Callières immediately contacted his brother in the homeland. ("Immediately" in those days quite often meant several months as a message had to go overland on foot and downstream by canoe before it reached a ship that would sail for France some time within a month or six weeks; and if the messenger missed the ship there would probably not be another for two or three months or longer.) The brother in question had, it seemed, some influence with the King and the Foreign Minister, having worked closely with them on the negotiations of the Peace of Ryswick. In a private interview with His Majesty, the brother asked for the post of Governor-General of New France for Louis. The request was granted.

De Callières' commission as Governor arrived in Quebec by the first ship to come from France in the spring of 1699. To compensate de Vaudreuil for his disappointment he was appointed Governor of Montreal, succeeding de Callières.

The haughty bearing of the new Governor was almost more than his associates could endure and the result of it was that, at first, he got little co-operation from any of them, except by direct command. As the months passed, however, it became apparent that he knew precisely what he was about in all phases of his new position, and soon he came to be regarded with a sincere though grudging admiration. With a finesse and capability that equalled Frontenac's, he tied up the unfinished ends of business with the Indians, a task made all the more hazardous since the Iroquois had become more daring upon learning of the death of Comte de Frontenac.

Peace parley followed peace parley. Upon one such occasion, at which de Callières had consented to smoke the pipe of peace around the Indian camp fire, the Governor rose from his ungraceful squatting position on a heap of furs and, with all the dignity of bearing permitted by his gouty feet and aching limbs, announced in grandiloquent style, "I bury the hatchet in a deep hole and over the hole I place a great rock, and over the rock I turn a river, that the hatchet may never be dug up again."

PORTRAIT OF CHAMPLAIN
ASCRIBED TO MONCORNET
FROM LAVERDIÈRE'S
CHAMPLAIN

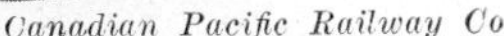

Canadian Pacific Railway Co.

Canadian Pacific Railway Co.

THE GRANDE HERMINE
PETITE HERMINE AND EMERILLON
IN THE ST. LAWRENCE, 1535

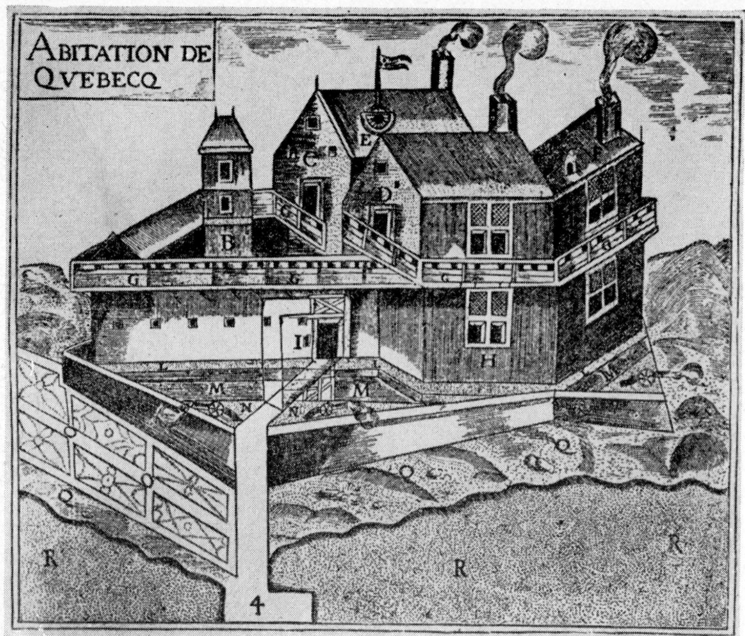

Public Archives of Canada

CHAMPLAIN'S HABITATION

THE MALTA STONE
IN THE COURTYARD OF
THE CHÂTEAU FRONTENAC

Associated Screen News Ltd.

PLAN OF
FORT ST. LOUIS,
QUEBEC, 1683, BY
JEAN-BAPTISTE
FRANQUELIN

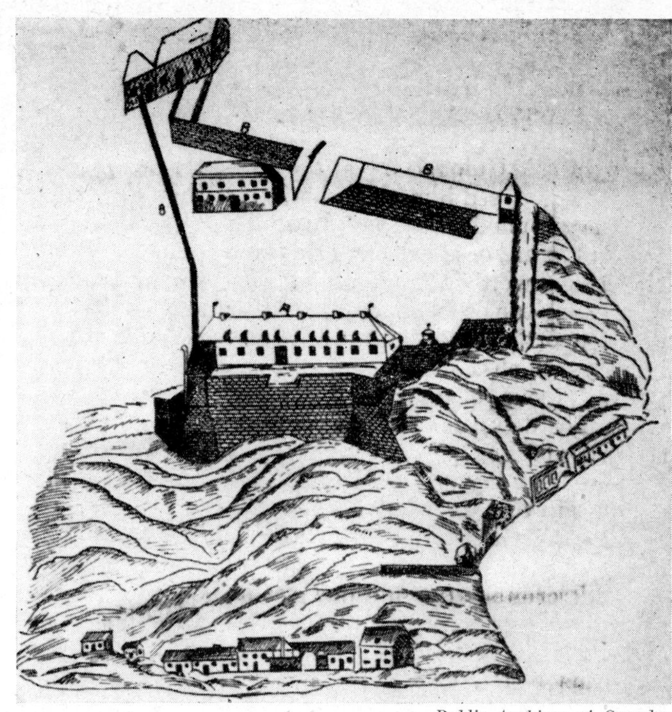

Public Archives of Canada

anadian Pacific Railway Co.

CHÂTEAU ST. LOUIS, QUEBEC

PLAN I.

CHATEAU S^T LOUIS. QUEBEC.

1723

From the Plans made and signed by
Chaussegros De Léry
July 10th 1724.

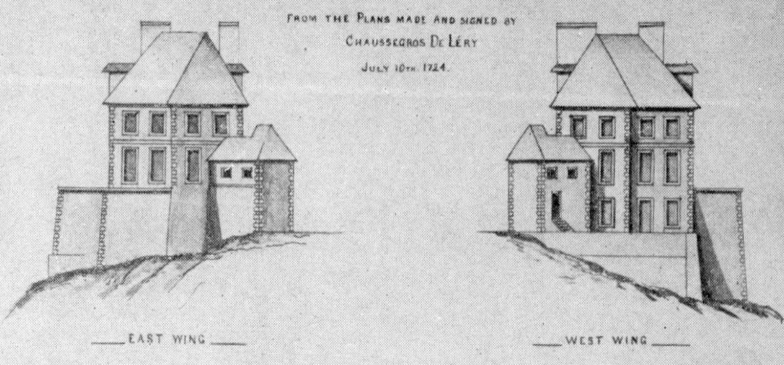

P.M. O'Leary Pxt.

Public Archives of Canada

FRONTENAC:
FROM PHOTOGRAPH
BY PHILIPPE HEBERT

Public Archives of Canada

ANNE DE LA GRANGE-TRIANON,
COMTESSE DE FRONTENAC*

Public Archives of Canada

**A copy of this painting hangs in the Château Frontenac*

Public Archives of Canada

CHÂTEAU ST. LOUIS

Public Archives of Canada

CHÂTEAU ST. LOUIS, RECONSTRUCTED BY FRONTENAC, 1694-1698; FINISHED IN 1700.

LE "VIEUX CHÂTEAU" (HALDIMAND HOUSE, 1784)

Public Archives of Canada

An exchange of prisoners then took place. The Indian captives gladly rejoined their tribes. Not so the French captives. Many of them had fared well among the Indians, had adopted their mode of life, had taken squaws for wives, and no longer wished to return to civilization. All of which proves—if anything—that it is easier to *un*-civilize a man than to civilize him.

The treaty was strengthened by a further agreement on the part of the French that they would pay the Indians the same prices for their furs as were paid by the English. Never again were the Indians to be a dominant power in New France. The New World had been wrested from their hands by force and with bloodshed, by fair means and foul,—and by those who felt they had a better right to it!

All through the years, now that the English had entrenched themselves so solidly in the south, there was fear among the people of the north that their city on the rock would again, sooner or later, be attacked by Britain. So de Callières set about putting the fortifications in good condition to withstand invasion. Unfortunately, he had scarcely begun this most necessary work when his gout and dropsy became too much for him and he died from a severe attack. While attending high Mass in the Cathedral on Ascension Day, 1703, he was taken with a vomiting of blood. He died in the Château St. Louis a few days later. He was buried in the Church of the Recollets.[5]

Too much of good could never be said for this wise man who took up the unenviable task of replacing one who had been loved, admired, respected and revered. De Callières was widely mourned. His personal life seems to have been colourless, with no wife to lighten his cares, and no lovely or lively ladies passing through the pleasant rooms of the old Château St. Louis. He seemed to suffer one attack of gout after another. This affliction was coupled with a constant worry as to how to make ends meet; his income from the Home Government was insufficient for his expenses; and the demands of his office made enormous and alarming inroads on his personal fortune. King Louis of France was far too busy building palaces and châteaux for his successive mis-

[5]Mr. P. G. Roy gives the date of death as May 26th, 1703. *Op. cit.*

tresses, and lavish sunken gardens for his favourites, giving outrageously opulent functions of every imaginable sort for any ridiculous reason, to be the least concerned over the repeated requests from the insignificant governor of a still more insignificant country!

****

Now it was de Vaudreuil's turn to become Governor of New France. He made the very most, to say the least, of the twenty-two years he held the position. At first he had suffered sharp embarrassment because of the doubt whether the appointment would be ratified because the King felt called upon to consider the social status of de Vaudreuil's wife which was somewhat below that of the governor-elect. The Marquise had been born Louise Elizabeth Joybert de Lotbinière, the daughter of M. Chartier De Lotbinière of Acadia, on the St. John river. It was feared that this alliance would impair the influence and authority of de Vaudreuil in his task of governor of all New France. Luckily, de Pontchartrain, the Foreign Minister, was in favour of the appointment and the objection was overruled. Some years later, when de Vaudreuil had incurred the Minister's displeasure over some trifling matter, de Pontchartrain wrote him on June 9th, 1706,

> "I must observe to you here that His Majesty felt some difficulty in resolving to confer on you the Governor-Generalship of New France, on account of your wife's family, which is now in that country, and His Majesty only consented on the assurance I have given him, that you would act towards your wife's relations as if they were no connection of yours. Should you depart from these principles, you will expose me to His Majesty's reproaches, and you ought even to be apprehensive for the consequences."

It was of no avail to try to impress the King with the fact that Louise de Lotbinière was the god-daughter of the Comte de Frontenac and thereby had some claim to distinction. However, the years were to reveal that the Marquise de Vaudreuil was a lady of excellent character and undeniable talents. On a visit to France in 1709, she so impressed the King that he made her Under-Governess to the Royal children. She attracted much attention at the Court of Versailles for her charm of manner and wit, not to mention her prudent behaviour in that world gone vulgarly mad. She did not return to Canada until 1716, when she accompanied her husband on his return from a visit to France where he had taken two years much-needed rest. Versailles had taught the Marquise many useful things.

De Vaudreuil's career is characterized by the raids he sponsored on the New England settlements with the aid of the Indians. If he achieved success in extending the power of New France, it was done through horror and bloodshed. He possessed little pretension to statesmanship, and his efforts were spurred simply by his fear of encroachment by the English.

The population of New England at this time was more than one hundred thousand; in the province of New York alone there were over thirty thousand persons. In all New France there were little more than fifteen thousand persons at the close of the seventeenth century. No wonder de Vaudreuil was apprehensive.

On February 29th, 1704, he sponsored the disgraceful attack on Deerfield, Massachusetts, during which many of its inhabitants were killed or taken prisoner. Governor Dudley of Massachusetts wrote de Vaudreuil that, although he had expected war, he had also expected "that it would be waged in accordance with the Christian beliefs and not against poor peasants, women and children". But this reproach in the name of humanity did not in any way deter the activities of de Vaudreuil in his zeal to protect New France. To him, the English settlers were simply biding their time to make an attack on the possessions of France, a scheme which he would be clever enough to foil before it had a chance.

Four years after the attack on Deerfield, de Vaudreuil caused another outstanding and devastating attack to be made on his white enemy to the south. The settlement of Haverhill was ravaged on August 29th, 1708, and this peaceful place, which had never given any cause for aggression, was all but wiped out of existence. It really began to look as if the English colonists would mildly accept any kind of treatment, no matter how brutal or undeserved. But, in 1709, the governors of the English provinces took stock of their resources and, upon receipt of promises of aid from England, discussed plans for reprisals. Colonel Francis Nicholson collected fifteen hundred men at Albany and placed his line of attack on Montreal *via* Lake Champlain. That was as far as the plans got. The whole idea collapsed. A ship arrived from England in October and brought information that the promised troops from home had been necessarily diverted to Portugal where, it was considered, more important issues were at stake.

Word of the danger that had threatened New France reached de Vaudreuil and, unaware that it had been dissipated, temporarily or otherwise, he began to strengthen the fortifications of Quebec and to coerce the undisciplined militia into some semblance of regular troops capable of engaging in a continuous campaign.

Once the excitement over the possibility of invasion had died, de Vaudreuil renewed his persecution of the smaller English settlements along the border. As a result, two years later the harassed people to the south put their heads together again and planned an ambitious expedition that would, once and for all time, end the French menace. It comprised five thousand troops from England and two thousand from the colonies, under Brigadier General Jack Hill. Part of this force was to go overland towards Montreal, *via* Lake Champlain, under General Francis Nicholson. The remainder was to go aboard the fleet commanded by Admiral Sir Hovenden Walker. The two forces were scheduled to converge on Quebec.

The fleet set sail from Boston on July 30th, 1711. It consisted of fifteen ships of war, forty-six transports, two bomb ketches, several hospital ships and storeships, all laden with men, ammunition and supplies for lengthy operations. All were in high spirits, for such was their strength that success seemed to them a foregone conclusion. Failure was the very last thing anticipated . . . until dense fog enveloped them in the gulf of St. Lawrence and spread its opaque curtain before their eyes, obliterating the islands in the vicinity as well as the treacherous shoals that surrounded each island, and preventing the advance towards Quebec.

Because there was but a handful of pilots in the whole armada, and they were incompetent, the ships were becalmed off the coast of Gaspe for three days; by the time they had regained their bearings and moved on, it was the 21st of August. They were scarcely out in the stream again when the fog came down thicker than before and they crept along on the windless sea until they realized they were off their course,—exactly thirty miles off.

It was the night of the 22nd that tragedy overtook them.

The Admiral, with inexplicable disregard for danger, had calmly retired to his cabin, and was clad only in his dressing-gown when one of his men entered his quarters and urged him to come on deck. The man had been scared out of his wits by the only real pilot aboard,—a Frenchman by the name of Paradis,—who had told him the truth of their position.

The very presence of Paradis on board was ironic. He and his ship had been taken prisoner by Walker in the Gulf and he was being forced, under threat of death, to guide the enemy against his own people. The story of this man has it that, while he realized the responsibility for human life placed in his hands, as well as the danger to himself, he was, at the same time, possessed of a natural desire to wreck the fleet to save Quebec. He guided them along the little-charted channel to the best of his ability however, and it is said that the disaster that overtook them was not due to deliberate intention on his part.

Paradis had his own means of undermining this expedition. He told the gullible Admiral and his lieutenants so many preposterous tales of the hazards that lay ahead of them in this venture that, at last, the Admiral concluded that the capture of Quebec was almost an impossible feat, situated as the City was upon unscalable heights. In his journal he wrote, "That which now chiefly took up my thoughts was contriving how to secure the ships if we got up to Quebec, for the ice in the river freezing to the bottom would have utterly destroyed and bilged them as much as if they had been squeezed between rocks."

Amazing though it is to record, Walker sat back in his elegant dressing-gown that night and actually laughed at the men who came to warn him of his danger. Three times they dared to disturb his rest with reiterated warnings.

"For the lord's sake, come on deck or we shall certainly be lost. There are breakers all around us."

Finally, in exasperation, Walker gave orders to steer to the north.

"Not to the north, Sir . . .!"

Once again the men appealed to him in terror. They could now see the shore, they said. This brought the Admiral on deck—in his dressing-gown and slippers. But it was too late for his counter orders to be effectively received and acted upon by all the ships. Eight of his precious transports with their even more precious human cargo sailed straight to destruction on the reefs of Egg Island, near Anticosti. Over seven hundred lives were lost.[6]

If we are to believe the tale as told by Charlevoix, who did not arrive in New France until ten years after this incident and must therefore have recorded it from reports given to him, there were three thousand bodies lying on the beach when the fog cleared away the next day.[7] All historians do not, by any means, agree with Charlevoix in these figures.

There was still a chance that the land force under Nicholson, together with what was left of the armada, could bring the expedition to a successful conclusion. New France was, generally speaking, poorly armed, manned and fortified; she could not look to France for help. France refused to send ships and men only to have them seized *en route* by the English.

But Sir Hovenden Walker had had quite enough of the whole affair. Without further ado, he salvaged what he could from the debacle and made an ignoble retreat to England. When the news reached Nicholson that the Admiral had withdrawn, he tore his hair, waved his hands wildly, and stamped about shouting like a madman. Yet he could do nothing himself but retreat.

One of Quebec's own twentieth-century historians, Colonel William Wood, has worded a choice paragraph which caustically sums up the incident:

> "An overwhelming joint expedition had come out under a mule of an admiral, Sir Hovenden Walker, and an ass of a general, known as Jack Hill. Walker gave order to 'keep it at north' till nine ships and 700 lives were lost on the northwest corner of the Gulf. And then, although there still was ample force to take Quebec, the ass and the mule brayed hard together and went home."[8]

[6] and [7]Historians vary in giving the number of lives lost in this expedition. The author has found that scarcely two are in accord.

[8]Colonel William Wood in *The Storied Province of Quebec, Past and Present.*

If one is interested in following the career of the incompetent mule, one will find that his world fell about his ears on his return to England. Contumely, derision, and disgrace were heaped upon Hovenden Walker and, in an attempt to vindicate himself, he wrote a lengthy account of the expedition which only added further to the scorn in which he was held. In this journal we find the following remarks, apropos of his thoughts after giving up the expedition, which describe his ideas of New France: "How dismal it must have been to have beheld the seas and earth locked up by adamantine frosts, and swoln with high mountains of snow, in a barren and uncultivated region; great numbers of brave men famishing with hunger and drawing lots who should die first to feed the rest."

On reading this, one is inclined to remark that Walker must have been under the impression, and rightly so, that the French of Canada were indeed a hardy race, and, further, that the mariner, Paradis, had done his job well.

England has never had any use for cowards—particularly when they were her own! The admiral, an admiral no longer, was stripped of his title and ordered out of the country. His name was struck from the naval lists. He went to America and settled for a short time in Carolina, where he soon found his circumstances unbearable and moved to the West Indies. He died in the Barbados, a broken and embittered man.

The news of the English fleet's disaster did not reach Quebec until October, and then New France rejoiced and thanked God through every saint for deliverance . . . and the Château St. Louis still raised its slate-grey roofs, undisturbed, to the benevolent sky.

❧❧❧❧❧❧❧❧❧❧❧❧

The Treaty of Utrecht, signed on March 31st, 1713, brought to an end the war with England, and King Louis of France was most grateful for it. He was old now. His lush living had brought on fatigue, a mortal weariness and feebleness—as well as a bankrupt treasury. It didn't matter much to him—but he had lost Acadia.

In the castle on the cliff in the New World, Governor de Vaudreuil was relaxing a little after the "wars and rumours of wars" that had beset him and his colonies for the past decade.

He rested to the extent of taking two years vacation in France, from whence he had returned bringing his lovely wife to grace the less elaborate court at Quebec. His very able and reliable commandant, M. de Ramezay, had administered the affairs of New France in his absence. Madame de Vaudreuil had been warmly welcomed back in her native land, but she remained in Quebec only until the death of her husband in 1725.

In September, 1712, the Intendancy had changed hands, Claude Michel Bégon replacing M. Raudot. This position was now one of vast power and influence and very little went on in the colony which was not known to the Intendant.

Quebec grew and throve in the years of peace between 1713 and 1725. De Vaudreuil encouraged industry, ship-building, and immigration. He alleviated the injustices that hampered manufacturing. Previous to 1706, the colonists were forbidden to manufacture cloth from their own home-grown hemp and flax; they were compelled to ship it to France where it was shoddily woven, returned to Canada, and sold back to the colonists at fabulous prices. In 1723, the hitherto undreamed of number of nineteen ships, built in Canada, sailed from the bustling port of Quebec.

De Vaudreuil urged that additional colonists be sent from France. A few hardy pioneers managed to cross the sea each year from the provinces of Normandie, Aunis, Perche, Poitou, Champagne, Picardie, Bretagne and Saintonge. The parishes of Quebec, a great number of which still retain their original boundaries in the immediate vicinity of the city, owe their well-chosen lines to the careful divisions laid out by this zealous governor. His life was rich in accomplishment. If he is to be condemned for his persistence in harassing the English colonies within his reach, he may be excused in that those were his orders, deemed necessary to protect his colony. He had built forts to the west to prevent enemy expansion in that direction and he considered it imperative to keep his enemy to the south weak and helpless lest eyes be turned covetously on the unpopulated west.

For twenty-two years de Vaudreuil watched conscientiously over the welfare of New France. He was eighty years of age when, overburdened by a strange mental depression, he took his well-earned rest and quietly died in his château on October 10th, 1725. He was deeply and sincerely lamented for he had been good to his people and had made himself very popular with them.

The Marquise de Vaudreuil, though now sixty-seven years old, still possessed vast influence with the French court, gained through her own intelligence and energy. She returned to France a few weeks after her husband's death, resumed her old place at court, and was given the position of governess to the children of the Duke de Berry. She lived in Paris until her death in January, 1740.[9]

Four sons had been born to the de Vaudreuils. One was destined to be the last French governor of New France.

✠✠✠✠✠✠✠✠✠✠✠✠

[9]P. G. Roy in *La Ville de Québec sous le Régime Français.*

Chapter Six

NOW IT SEEMED THAT peace had, for a change, decided to favour French Canada. The lovely St. Lawrence swept leisurely on to the sea undisturbed by enemy squadrons. The humble peasants along its shores went contentedly about the business of wresting a livelihood in a primitive land; and their labours began to bear fruit in improved living conditions.

Substantial buildings also testified to the diligence and toil of the people. In the vicinity of the Château St. Louis could be seen, at the opening of the eighteenth century, a splendid palace for the Bishop, a College for the Jesuits, a prosperous convent for the Ursulines, an inspiring Cathedral, and the Hôtel Dieu for the sick. These buildings were irregularly placed in relation to each other, and had to be reached by winding roads that certainly bore no resemblance to city streets, being always damp and sticky from countless springs, but this was Canada's first city—built upon a hill, founded on a rock.

The scattered grouping of the colonists' homes bore testimony, too, to the nature of the rock upon which they were built. In those days, one built one's house where the rock permitted, for the rock was immovable and impenetrable.

✽✽✽✽✽✽✽✽✽✽✽

The new Governor, M. Charles de Beauharnois, a naval officer of fifty-six years of age, did not arrive in Quebec until August 30th, 1726.[1] He was unmarried, as far as can be ascertained. He was accompanied to Quebec by M. Claude Dupuy, the new Intendant.

In the interim between the death of de Vaudreuil and the arrival of de Beauharnois, the government had been administered quite ably by a French-Canadian, the Baron de Longueuil, Governor of Montreal. He had solicited the position of Governor-General for himself but, unfortunately, lacked the required influence with the French Court to bring it about.

[1]P. G. Roy, *La Ville de Québec sous le Régime Français.*

For twenty-one years de Beauharnois guided the affairs of New France to its advantage and to his own credit. Because there was peace, greater progress was made in the City on the rock than ever before in any comparative period in its history. New France was becoming a land where a house and a few acres of good soil augured a most desirable future. Of course, the climate was stern, especially in winter. Food was not lavish, and there was little pleasure. But, with the produce of summer carefully laid away for the snowbound months, the inhabitants gave vent to their naturally vivacious good spirits and many a long winter evening was spent in lively conversation, dancing to a violin, making taffy, telling tales of home and of adventures in the forests of New France. No longer did the people live in fear of war whoops echoing all too near their homes and loved ones. . . . For this they repeatedly thanked Heaven and a certain "fighting governor" who had recently gone to rest in the Cathedral. The population of New France had increased to fifty thousand.

In 1727, Quebec suffered the loss of the good Bishop St. Vallier, who died on December 26th. His successor was Monseigneur Louis-François de Mornay, who, though Bishop of Quebec until 1733, never came to New France. The reason given by his contemporaries is that he was afraid of the sea.[2]

Bishop de Mornay was succeeded by Monseigneur Pierre-Herman Dosquet, who was resident Bishop in Quebec for a year, returning to France in 1735. He, in turn, was succeeded by Monseigneur Louis Pourroy de Lauberivière, who was replaced in 1741 by Monseigneur Henri-Marie du Breuil de Pontbriand, who died at Montreal in 1760.

In 1728, the Intendant Dupuy released the Intendancy, which office he had discharged very weakly, to M. Giles Hocquart who was appointed by the King as *commissaire-général de la Marine*.[3] Hocquart has been justly referred to as the only Intendant whose abilities and accomplishments were worthy of comparison with the great Talon. He left Canada in the autumn of 1748.

❋❋❋❋❋❋❋❋❋❋❋❋

The birth of the Dauphin of France on September 4th, 1729,

[2]and[3]P. G. Roy, *Op. cit.*

was not known in Quebec until April 1st of the following year. The arrival of the news touched off a series of celebrations in honour of the heir to the throne of the Motherland. Following as he did three sisters, the heir to the throne of France was welcomed with great rejoicing and satisfaction among the people.[4] The seven-months long celebrations at Quebec in honour of this new arrival centered in and about the Governor's château. There was a gun salute from the fort which was followed by the ringing of all the bells in the town and services in all the churches. In the evening the Governor gave a great banquet in the Château St. Louis.

On July 31st, 1730, a ship from France brought the official announcement of the birth of the dauphin, and this started the celebrations all over again. There were processions from the Château St. Louis to the Cathedral and back again, which were accompanied by the booming of cannon from the Fort. Bonfires were lit in the squares and the militia was drawn up in order of battle, and as the fires burned higher the town rang with shouts of *Vive le Roi!* Across the river, on the cliffs facing Quebec, fireworks illuminated the evening sky and the words *Vive le Roi* were spelt out in glowing lights. A splendid banquet was held that night in old Château St. Louis, and toasts were drunk to the King, the Queen, and their royal son. Dancing followed, which lasted well into the night.

The last fête for the dauphin was held on October 15th, 1730. The citizens then returned to the business of living, still a most real and earnest matter in this new land.

The early years of the 1730's were marked, in New France, by earthquakes, floods, famine, and disease. The earthquakes frightened the people almost out of their wits; there were still a few among them who could recall the terrible year 1663. The floods of the St. Lawrence laid waste their lands; famine weakened them and smallpox killed them relentlessly, reducing their numbers as nothing had ever done before. Disease and the scarcity of food were an overpowering combination. People were forced to eat horsemeat, varied with a little codfish, with a ration of four

[4]The Dauphin never became King; he died in 1765, before the death of his father, but he had married and had three sons, each of whom became king in turn, Louis XVI, Louis XVIII, Charles X. (P. G. Roy, *Op. cit.*)

ounces of bread daily, and rarely anything else. Frequently people fell in the streets from weakness, and died of hunger.[5]

It is reported that three hundred people died of smallpox in Montreal alone, and as many more in Quebec.[6] By 1739 the population of New France had been reduced to forty-two thousand seven hundred.

****

It is believed that de Beauharnois built the wing to the Château St. Louis which La Potherie had reported as lacking in 1698.[7] No other improvements for the historic pile of stone which dominated the French world in North America have been recorded during de Beauharnois' term.

In 1745 Britain's Royal Navy took Louisbourg in Acadia from the French, thereby enraging the French government. In seeking someone on whom to place the blame the government considered the governor of New France at fault and recalled him. On March 15th, 1746, the Marquis de la Jonquière was appointed to replace him.

Charles de Beauharnois left Quebec on October 14th, 1747.[8] However, as he was made a lieutenant-general in the navy upon his return to France, he must have been able to explain satisfactorily any charges laid against him regarding his responsibility for the loss of Louisbourg.

This governor's life seems to have been very unobtrusive. In 1716 he married Renée Pays Hardouineau, widow of Pierre Hardouineau, of the seigniory of Laudianière. She was of an advanced age, and no children were born of their marriage. The belief has been expressed that she died before he came to New France.[9] De Beauharnois died in Paris on July 12th, 1749.[10]

A great-nephew of de Beauharnois, Alexandre de Beauharnois, was the first husband of the Empress Josephine before Napoleon I discovered her.[11]

****

[5]F. X. Garneau, *History of Canada.*
[6]Dr. William Kingsford in *History of Canada, Vol. III.*
[7]See Chapter V of *Castle of Quebec.*
[8]Date given by P. G. Roy in *La Ville de Québec sous le Régime Français.*
[9] [10]and[11]P. G. Roy, *Op. cit.*

In the hope of regaining her losses in Acadia, France sent out, in April, 1747, six ships of the line and thirty transports, laden with troops and equipment, under Admiral Jacques Pierre Taffanel, Marquis de la Jonquière. After taking Louisbourg, la Jonquière was to continue on to Quebec with his new commission to assume the government of New France. The third of May found the French fleet engaged in a losing battle with the British navy, which resulted in the French fleet being captured and the governor taken to England as a prisoner, where he was held for two years.

But war or no war, New France had to have a royal representative, and so Rolland Michel Barrin, Comte de la Galissonière, was appointed administrator, and arrived in Quebec on September 19th, 1747. He was a distinguished gentleman of fifty-four years of age. In appearance he is said to have been slightly deformed; not so his character, of which nothing but good can be said. He was very well educated, and during his two-year term of office in New France he was unremitting in his efforts to enlighten the people. He proved his statesmanship in his attempts to define the boundaries between New France and New England, advocating that the line should follow the Allegheny Mountains, and that the English should be confined to the seaboard and barred from the interior. He strengthened the forts to the West, and built new ones at Green Bay, Ogdensburg and York.

For some years the Comte had been an associate member of the Royal Academy of Natural Sciences, and while in New France went to great pains to foster an interest in the plant and animal life of the country. He sent out lengthy circulars to all his officers in their outposts, advising them that he wished them to collect and send specimens to France of the natural products of the country.

La Galissonière's efforts in this sphere were given impetus by a distinguished visitor whom he entertained most royally at the Château St. Louis. He was the famous Swedish botanist, Professor Peter Kalm who arrived in Quebec on August 5th, 1749.[12]

Kalm is outstanding among world travellers who have kept journals as they moved. Accredited by academies and universities,

[12] J. M. Le Moine, *Glimpses of Quebec during the Last Ten years of French Dominion, 1749-1759.*

commended by the kings of Sweden and France, Kalm has left us beautiful word pictures of the city of Quebec, the country of New France, the people and the customs. He spent about forty days in Quebec where, after a few days as a guest of the Governor in his Château, he lived in lodgings at the home of a Madame Lajus.

Of Quebec, Kalm wrote, "The mountain, on which the upper city is situated, reaches above the houses of the lower city. Notwithstanding the latter are three or four stories high, and the view, from the palace, of the lower city (part of which is immediately under it) is enough to cause a swimming of the head. There is only one easy way of getting to the upper city, and there part of the mountain has been blown up. This road is very steep, notwithstanding it is made winding and serpentine. However, they go up and down it in carriages and with waggons. All the other roads up the mountain are so steep that it is very difficult to climb to the top of them. Most of the merchants live in the lower city, where the houses are built very close together. The streets in it are narrow, very rugged, and almost always wet. There is likewise a church, and a small marketplace. The upper city is inhabited by people of quality, by several persons belonging to the different offices, by tradesmen, and others. In this part are the chief buildings of the town, among which the following are worthy of particular notice: 1. The Palace (Château St. Louis) is situated on the west or steepest side of the mountain, just above the lower city. It is not properly a palace, but a large building of stone, two stories high, extending north and south. On the west side of it is a court yard, surrounded partly with a wall, and partly with houses. On the east side, or towards the river, is a gallery as long as the whole building, and about two fathom broad, paved with smooth flags, and included on the outsides by iron rails, from whence the city and the river exhibit a charming prospect. This gallery serves as a very agreeable walk after dinner, and those who come to speak with the governor-general wait here till he is at leisure. The palace is the lodging of the governor-general of Canada, and a number of soldiers mount the guard before it, both at the gate and in the court yard; and when the governor, or the bishop, comes in or goes out, they must all appear in arms, and beat the drum."[13]

[13]Peter Kalm, *Travels in North America.*

The Marquis de la Jonquière arrived belatedly in Quebec on August 14th, 1749. La Galissonière returned to France, resumed his naval career and won great glory by defeating Admiral Byng at Minorca. He died at Nemours, October 26th, 1756.

By the time La Jonquière reached Quebec—released by a peace between England and France which was, as so often, scarcely more than a truce—he was sixty-three years of age, and his health was not too robust. His character, as reported by history, seems to have been of a most contradictory nature. We read that he loved public ceremony and its attendant splendour; that he was extremely parsimonious and frugal; and so poorly educated as to know little of the etiquette and courtesies expected of a man in his position.

La Jonquière's debarkation and entry into Quebec are described by Professor Kalm (who was an eye-witness to the proceedings, having been invited to accompany the officials at the welcome) as a most sumptuous display. La Galissonière, who had not yet left for France, was on hand to officiate at the welcome. The new Governor created something of a sensation in his costume of royal scarlet and gold, his chest laden with decorations. His entourage was equally as dazzling. He swept along with great style and dignity as if he had never known the inside of an English prison. Every cannon in the Fort boomed; every bell in the city clanged. After the customary service in the Cathedral the formal presentation to the new Governor of the keys of the citadel took place. This was followed by a festive *soirée* in the Château St. Louis.

During La Jonquière's term of office there appeared on the scene a man who, with consummate skill, began to weave a web of embezzlement and chicanery unparalleled in the history of New France—indeed, comparable to any of its kind the world has ever known! His name: François Bigot. He replaced the excellent Hocquart as Intendant in 1748. There is some doubt as to whether La Jonquière was involved in Bigot's illegal enterprises. We only know that he loved money to excess, was unscrupulous in his methods of obtaining it, and that he collected immense sums.

In his dealing with the clergy, La Jonquière was openly

defiant of them. They had forbidden the trade in brandy but the Governor dealt as he pleased. The Jesuits complained to France, but France was weary of New France and her constant demands. Considerable sums had been spent to fortify the stronghold of Quebec, and there was always an outstanding request for more money. Then there were the reports that the people of Quebec were near starvation. King Louis demanded an accounting. None was forthcoming that could be called satisfactory, so France began to toy with the idea that New France might well be abandoned.

At this point La Jonquière showed wisdom. He resigned active management of the country's affairs into the hands of Charles Le Moyne,[14] Baron de Longueuil, Governor of Montreal, who watched over the country until a new governor should arrive.

La Jonquière had married Marie-Angélique de la Valette in 1721, by whom he had one daughter, but neither accompanied him to New France. He died in the spring of 1752, aged sixty-seven, and was buried in the church of the Recollets in Quebec.

The city of Pittsburgh was once called Fort Duquesne. It was established by Michel Ange Duquesne-Menneville, Marquis de Duquesne, eighteenth governor of New France. In the hands of the French, in its strategic position at the juncture of the Allegheny and Monongahela Rivers, it was a formidable outpost threatening any English who dared encroach upon its territory.

History tells us very little about Duquesne. He arrived in Quebec in the summer of 1752. We do not know if he brought a wife to Canada, or even if he was married. Of his character, we know that he was rather lonely, somewhat irritable, and that he had no friends and sought none.[15] He was a naval man of distinguished family.

Duquesne's attention was first drawn to the state of the militia in Quebec, which was very lax in discipline and badly needed training. The Governor undertook to coerce the soldiers into some sort of usefulness, and his severe tactics in this connection won him great unpopularity among the military, as well as the ire of the

[14]Le Moyne is the early French spelling. In later usage it became Le Moine.
[15]P. G. Roy, *La Ville de Québec sous le Régime Français.*

thieving Intendant Bigot who claimed that the military training took the men too much from the soil.

Duquesne was extremely proud and haughty, and he ignored the Intendant as if he were non-existent. Therein may lie the reason behind the fact that Duquesne never became involved, willingly or otherwise, in Bigot's unscrupulous maladministration.

During the opening months of 1755 it began to look as if war would once more be declared between France and England. Duquesne, a navy man to the core, sent in his resignation as governor of New France, and requested a naval appointment. He returned to France where he distinguished himself still further and was rewarded by being made a Commander of the Order of St. Louis. He died at Antony, Seine, on September 17th, 1778.

Chapter Seven

On Abram's Plains the storm of battle grew,
As night his shadowy mantle round him drew,
And fled, affrighted . . .

W. F. HAWLEY.

IT WAS NOT UNTIL May 18th, 1756, that war was actually declared on England by France and by that time Pierre de Vaudreuil, fourth son of Philippe de Vaudreuil, a former governor, was firmly esconced in the Château St. Louis as Governor of all New France. He had arrived in Quebec on June 23rd, 1755, directly from his post as Governor of Louisiana, which territory was still in French hands.

The Marquis de Vaudreuil-Cavagnal was the first of the French-Canadians as we know them today. No ties with France blinded him to the welfare of New France. He had been born and raised in the territory over which he now governed, and *la nouvelle France* not *l'ancienne France* was his first consideration. Had he lived in a peaceful era, de Vaudreuil-Cavagnal would doubtless have proven himself of inestimable value to the new generation of French-Canadians who were wondering if it might not be possible to exist apart from the motherland who had cared so little for her unwanted offspring. But fate decreed otherwise for this man. Or was he the master of his own destiny? The stage was set. He was to play the part of a jaundiced buffoon under the direction of artful men, a character too weak to exert the power he held over them and to play the role he might have played.

De Vaudreuil had to choose between two men and, because he chose wrongly, the curtain dropped darkly over him and over all New France. One of these men was François Bigot, a selfish scoundrel. The other was an honest soldier of fortune, Louis Joseph le Marquis de Montcalm-Gozon de Saint-Veran.

Of the scoundrel enough has already been said for the moment.

The Marquis de Montcalm was a man of superior mentality, education and breeding. He is described as a country gentleman, a man who loved his home and family, music and literature, and whose greatest desire was to enjoy them always. Francis Parkman describes him as "a man of small stature, with a lively countenance, a keen eye, and, in moments of animation, of rapid vehement utterance, and nervous gesticulation."[1] He was sent to New France to direct the campaigns being waged there against the English.

Montcalm was met by an antagonistic governor who took no pains to hide his bitterness that a Frenchman instead of a French-Canadian had been given military control in New France. On the other hand, we are told Montcalm did not like the Canadians, and could never humble himself to serve under them.[2] The two men disagreed in policy from the beginning, and when Montcalm became aware of the corruption within the colony, which apparently had de Vaudreuil's sanction if not his support, their dislike became mutual. The letters each wrote to France complaining of the other are amazing records of dissension in high places at a time when accord was imperative to the success of the cause.

De Vaudreuil wrote, "As the King has entrusted this colony to me, I cannot help warning you of the unhappy consequences that would follow if the Marquis de Montcalm should remain here. . . . I pass over in silence all the infamous conduct and indecent talk he has held or countenanced; but I should be wanting in my duty to the King if I did not beg you to ask for his recall."

It was obvious that these men disagreed as to how the war should be waged. Bougainville, a close friend of Montcalm, as well as one of the cleverest commanding officers of the French, wrote to a friend, "When de Vaudreuil produces an idea he falls in love with it, as Pygmalion did with his statue. I can forgive Pymalion for what he produced was a masterpiece!" Certainly de Vaudreuil produced no masterpieces of strategy!

When Montcalm wrote complaining of Bigot's activities, the Foreign Minister sent a copy of his letter to de Vaudreuil, who

[1]Francis Parkman. *Montcalm and Wolfe.*

[2]P. G. Roy, *La Ville de Québec sous le Régime Français.* "Montcalm . . . n'aimait pas les Canadiens . . . et il ne put jamais se plier à servir sous un Canadien."

explained to the Minister: "I cannot conceal from you, Monseigneur, how deeply M. Bigot feels the suspicions expressed in your letter. He does not deserve them, I am sure. He is full of zeal for the service of the King; but as he is rich, or passes as such, and as he has merit, the ill-disposed are jealous and insinuate that he has prospered at the expense of His Majesty. I am certain that it is not true, and that nobody is a better citizen than he, or has the King's interests more at heart." All this, in justification of a man who forced the people to sell all their produce to him at ridiculously low prices and paid them in notes that gradually depreciated in value until, in 1759, the Ministry of France declared them worthless, thereby rendering Quebec bankrupt, except for the vast private fortunes amassed by himself and his equally rapacious associates!

Such were conditions in Quebec when William Pitt of England commissioned a brilliant young officer, of thirty-four years of age, named James Wolfe, to lay siege to it as the keystone of French strength in America.

On February 15th, 1759, sixty transports, six ships of the line, and nine frigates left the harbour of Portsmouth, England. General Wolfe and Admiral Saunders were on board with an army of nine thousand men.

As the angelus rang gently over the humble homes of Quebec on the evening of June 26th, the English fleet came to anchor off the Island of Orleans. The siege of Quebec had begun. Surely the sight of the mighty cliffs of Quebec must have caused a qualm or two in the breasts of the invaders from the "tight little island"! But not the slightest disaster had befallen them on their cruise up the St. Lawrence river and they considered this augured well for the whole expedition.

Wolfe was fully as fine a character as his enemy, Montcalm, and Parkman describes him as "ardent, headlong, void of fear, often rash, almost fanatical in his devotion to military duty, and reckless of life when the glory of England or his own was at stake."[3] He was also good and kindly, utterly honest and forthright.

Wolfe was not married, but had come exceedingly near to that state on two different occasions. In biographies of this hero,

[3]Francis Parkman, *Montcalm and Wolfe.*

mention is made of two ladies who, one after the other, held a place in his heart. The first was Elizabeth Lawson, eldest daughter of Sir Wilfrid Lawson, and Maid of Honour to the Princess of Wales. This romance ended many years before the invasion of New France because the lady suffered from ill-health, even more so than Wolfe himself. She died shortly after Wolfe's departure for Quebec. But long before her death, Wolfe had fallen in love with lovely young Katherine Lowther, daughter of the erstwhile governor of Barbados, and a niece of the first Lord Lonsdale. Since she was an heiress and in the bloom of health, it was not long before they became engaged. When Wolfe departed for America, he carried an exquisite miniature of this lady in the pocket of his tunic. After his death, and in accordance with his instructions, it was set in a circlet of jewels and returned to her. An excerpt from Wolfe's Last Will and Testament reads:

> "Neptune at Sea
> 8th June, 1759.
>
> I desire that Miss Lowther's Picture may be set in jewels to the amount of Five Hundred Guineas, and returned to her."[4]

Just before Wolfe left England, Thomas Gray had written a new poem which he had called "Elegy in a Country Churchyard". It had caught Wolfe's fancy, and the story is told by the coxswain of the boat in which Wolfe passed the night of September 12th, 1759, before Quebec, that the General remarked that he would "rather have written that poem than take Quebec tomorrow."[5] It is said that Wolfe had a copy of this poem with him at Quebec. In 1913 a copy was found in Paris which bore the initials "K.L.". It is believed to be the copy that Wolfe carried with him to Quebec. If so, who took it to France? Was it taken immediately after the battle or many years later by someone who chanced upon it?

Montcalm was forty-four at this time and had been married long enough to have ten children. He was profoundly in love with his wife and wrote her the most tender letters during all his nerve-wracking campaigns. "The moment when I see you once

[4]As taken from John Knox's Journal edited by A. G. Doughty which reproduces the original.

[5]*The Quebec Mercury*, May 23rd, 1839.

more will be the brightest of my life," he wrote while he was doing his best to strengthen Quebec in case it should be attacked. At the height of the siege, when the town was slowly being blown to ruins all about him, he wrote longingly, "When shall I see my *château de Candiac*, my plantations, my chestnut grove, my oil-mill, my mulberry trees? *O bon Dieu. . . .*"

The story of how Wolfe surprised Quebec on the morning of September 13th, 1759, by the magnificent ascent of his army up the cliff of Cape Diamond (then considered unscalable) from the *Anse au Foulon* (since called Wolfe's Cove); how he led his troops in direct combat against the French troops led by Montcalm; how the two commanders were struck down almost simultaneously, forms a glorious annal in the history of Quebec—indeed, in the history of Canada and the Empire. It has left a halo of immortality about the names and memory of two of the bravest and noblest men who ever trod upon Canadian soil.

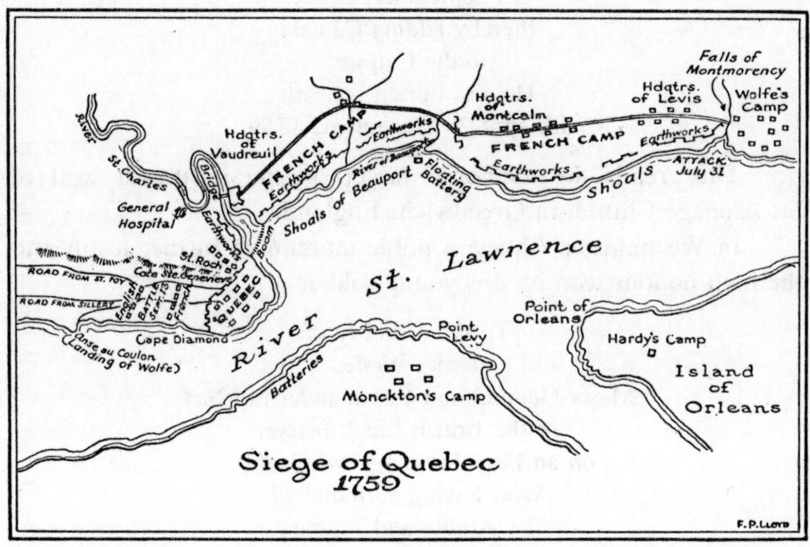

As Montcalm, mortally wounded but uncomplaining, struggled along St. Louis street in an effort to reach the shelter of the castle walls to die in peace, the fate of the Château St. Louis was decided. Though Wolfe had fallen, too, and lay dying on the edge of the battlefield, his armies had routed the French.

Meanwhile, de Vaudreuil-Cavagnal, some distance outside the city with reinforcements, heard of the retreat and, instead of ordering his fresh troops to attempt to retrieve the loss, he withdrew.

Four days later, at four o'clock in the afternoon, Quebec capitulated to the English in a solemn ceremony in Place d'Armes square. The flag of the Bourbons came down from above the roof of the Château St. Louis and was replaced by the Union Jack of Queen Anne.

✤✤✤✤✤✤✤✤✤✤✤✤

To the Glory of God
and to the Memory of
James Wolfe, Major-General.
Born at Westerham in Kent,
2 January, 1727.
Died Victorious
on the Heights above Quebec,
13 September, 1759,
thereby adding Canada
to the Empire.
He was buried beneath
this spot 20 November, 1759.

Thus reads the memorial tablet on the northwest wall of St. Alphege Church in Greenwich, England.

In Westminster Abbey, a noble monument further testifies to the high honour won by this young soldier:

To the Memory of
James Wolfe,
Major-General and Commander-in-Chief
of the British Land Forces,
on an Expedition against Quebec;
Who having surmounted
By Ability and Valour,
Was slain in the moment of Victory,
on the 13th of September, 1759.
The King and Parliament of Great Britain
dedicated this Monument.

On the edge of the battlefields on the Plains of Abraham, as near as could be determined to the spot where he breathed his last, Wolfe is commemorated with another stately monument. In 1832 such a column was erected by Lord Aylmer, but it suffered so seriously from the ravages of time and weather and the hands of souvenir hunters (who quickly made off with the pieces the weather obligingly crumbled from it) that, in 1849, the monument was removed and replaced by one of sturdier construction. The stones of the old were laid beneath the new monument. On it is the simple and expressive inscription:

Here Died
Wolfe
Victorious

The body of Montcalm had been buried in a rough, hastily constructed coffin placed in a shell hole made in the wall of the Ursuline Convent in Quebec. In 1833 his skull was exhumed and placed in a glass-enclosed cabinet in an apartment of the Chaplain of the Convent, where visitors may see it. In 1835 Lord Aylmer, then Governor-General of Canada, placed there a tablet which reads:

Honour to Montcalm
Destiny, in depriving him of Victory,
Recompensed him with a glorious Death.[6]

A monument to Montcalm looks down on the smart residential Grande Allée of Quebec. It bears the words:

Honneur
à
Montcalm
La France
Le Canada

It is said to have been a gift of the French Republic to Quebec in "honour of a great Frenchman".

And in order that the two races, who dwell peaceably together where once Frenchman fought Englishman, might have a

[6]Translated from the French wording as given in *Old Quebec, the Fortress of New France* by Gilbert Parker and Claude G. Bryan. "Honneur à Montcalm—Le Destin en Lui Derobant—La Victoire—L'a Récompensé par—Une Morte Glorieuse."

monument to their unity, a single splendid spire of stone, erected on the cliff in the shadow of the Château Frontenac, was unveiled in 1827 by Lord Dalhousie. On one side of it is the name Montcalm, on the opposite, Wolfe; on a third side, in a language neither French nor English but *Latin*, is inscribed:

Courage gave Them a Common Death
History a Common Fame
Posterity a Common Monument

On the fourth side, also in Latin, here translated:

The Foundation Stone of this Monument
in the Memory of the Illustrious Men,
Wolfe and Montcalm,
was laid by
George, Earl of Dalhousie,
Governor in Chief over all the British Provinces
in North America,
a work neglected for many years.
(What is there more worthy of a Gallant General?)
He promoted by his influence, encouraged by his example,
and favoured by his munificence.
15th November, 1827.
George IV, Reigning King of
Great Britain.

❊❊❊❊❊❊❊❊❊❊❊❊❊

The deposed Governor de Vaudreuil left Canada almost immediately after the capitulation. The Intendant Bigot and his accomplices were also summoned home. Upon their arrival in France both governor and intendant underwent the disgrace of a trial to determine their guilt or innocence in the misappropriation of funds and supplies in Quebec. In due time, de Vaudreuil was officially acquitted but the calumny of the charges was destined to cling forever to his name. Some reports tell us he died in Paris some eighteen years later almost friendless, mourned only by his wife, the former Charlotte Fleury de la Gorgendière. Still other reports say that King Louis pardoned him and gave him a pension of six thousand livres, and that he ordered a letter to be written to him in which he advised de Vaudreuil that he had been cleared of all reproaches, and besides the pension would receive the Grand Cross of the Order of St. Louis as a recompense for the indignities he had suffered through trial and imprisonment. It is highly possible that the whole truth was known to very few persons.

On December 10th, 1763, Bigot was found guilty on all charges laid against him and was subjected to a humiliation which must certainly have broken his vain, proud heart. On this all historians agree. Besides returning out of his personal fortune a large part of the misappropriated funds,[7] he was tied to the gate of the Bastille and forced to cry aloud his guilt in loud clear tones to passersby—after which he was exiled for life to Bordeaux.

As for France, what were her reactions to her loss of the "few acres of snow in Canada"?[8] A lavish banquet was held in the King's palace which was attended by all the kingdom's great, the royal favourites with their wives or mistresses; hearty toasts were drunk to the effect that France was indeed richer to be rid of New France since, from its discovery, it had been only a constant worry, as well as an alarming drain on the treasury.

The vituperous Voltaire, current court favourite, gave a sumptuous banquet at his home in Ferney, in honour of the event, and King Louis (XV) graced the table with his royal presence. The host, in his usual pertinent terms, congratulated his Royal Master on having "rid himself of those fifteen thousand arpents of snow so that now he (the King) would have a chance to sleep in peace"—which is surely the first intimation we have that anyone in France had lost any sleep worrying over New France!

Everyone in France forecast that Canada would prove not only a burden but an embarrassment to the conqueror. In this they were, unfortunately, all too correct. Canada *was* a burden and *did* prove an embarrassment to the English on many occasions for many years. Was she, argued the British politicians, really worth what she would undoubtedly cost the British government?

[7]P. G. Roy in *La Ville de Québec sous le Régime Français* says that Bigot's properties were confiscated, that he was fined one thousand livres and forced to pay one million five hundred thousand livres as restitution.

[8]Voltaire in *Candida.*

Chapter Eight

The star of even look'd on Britain's glory,
And saw a new wreath laid upon its shrine . . .
W. F. HAWLEY.

WOLFE HAD BEEN BURIED for four years beside his father in the family vault in St. Alphege Church, Greenwich; Montcalm had been resting in the walls of the Ursuline Convent, Quebec, an equal length of time, before the Treaty of Paris, which put an official end to the Seven Years War, was signed in 1763.

By this treaty, France renounced her claims on Acadia and Canada. England granted "to the inhabitants of Canada freedom of the Catholic religion, in so far as permitted by the laws of Great Britain"—but since the laws of Great Britain were, even at that time, somewhat restrictive where Catholics were concerned, and had yet to undergo radical changes to permit absolute freedom of worship within her own borders as well as in her colonies, there necessarily arose frequent dissension in Canada between conqueror and conquered.

It is not the point of this story to delve into the political or spiritual unrest that tore at the vitals of young Canada in the early days of British rule, or indeed at any time in her history, except in those specific instances where Church and State were inseparably linked with the Château St. Louis and its masters. It is sufficient at this moment to say that had it not been for the great wisdom, tact and understanding exhibited at all times by the first British representatives in Canada—General James Murray and Sir Guy Carleton—Canada might still have slipped from Britain's grasp.

General Murray remained in Canada as Governor for three years. He was replaced in 1766 by Sir Guy Carleton who was later to become Lord Dorchester. Both had served under Wolfe and had proven valorous in battle and wise in strategy. Their opinions had always been respectfully considered by young Wolfe.

Murray had resigned his position as Governor when he became aware of the disfavour he had engendered among the English-

Canadians by giving too much consideration to the French-Canadians. No doubt in his effort to be fair and just to a discouraged people, Murray had done precisely that for which he was condemned. He had won the love and gratitude of the French but had drawn only censure from the English. Certain French writers of the period, though deeply imbued with strong racial instincts and love for their Mother country, have written that they and the people were happy and satisfied under the laws of justice and citizenship as set up by the British. Dr. Labrie in his *Memoire Abbé Verrault* writes: "The officers of the troops were the administrators of justice, respecting always and even following in their procedures the laws and ancient customs of the colony, to the extent they knew them, or that circumstances permitted." One must add, however, that while authority for the enforcement of law was in the hands of the military it was by no means done at the bayonet's point.

The first act of Great Britain was to give permission to the French to leave the country if they wished to do so, or to remain in Canada. It was not altogether flattering to old France that the number who chose to return to her fold was less than three hundred, and that the rest preferred to stay where they were even though they would be under the rule of the hated British. But, after all, they had come alone to a strange land, and the Mother country had done little for them.

The difference in language brought about untold difficulties, particularly with regard to the laws. General Murray did everything possible to appease the taut-nerved, half-starved French-Canadians, and from the beginning advocated that English law should be followed in criminal instances only, since it was more humane than the French-Canadian law which still had recourse to the rack and the pillory; and that French law should prevail in civil cases as being best suited to the customs of the people.

In 1774 the Quebec Act was passed by the British Government incorporating the foregoing efforts to bring peace and harmony between the two peoples now in Canada and ". . . for the more perfect Security and Ease of the Minds of the Inhabitants of the said Province (Canada), it is hereby declared, That His Majesty's

Subjects, professing the Religion of the Church of Rome, ... may have, hold, and enjoy, the free Exercise of the Religion of the Church of Rome, subject to the King's Supremacy, ... that the Clergy of the said Church may hold, receive, and enjoy, their accustomed Dues and Rights, with respect to such Persons only as shall profess the said Religion . . . . (and) Whereas the Certainty and Lenity of the Criminal Law of England, and the Benefits and Advantages resulting from the use of it, have been sensibly felt by the Inhabitants, from an Experience of more than Nine Years, during which it has been uniformly administered; be it therefore enacted . . . . that the same shall continue to be administered. . . ."

Murray had faced a monumental task. Besides pacifying current disagreements and working out a government capable of conducting the affairs of the country, he had undertaken to regulate the supply and price of grain, meat and bread, and to establish the value of the current coin in both French and English. And he had found Quebec in ruins. "A hundred and eighty houses had been burned, and most of the others had suffered from shot. . . . The Cathedral had been entirely burned. The church of the Lower Town had been demolished. The chapels of the Recollets, the Jesuits, and the seminary, had undergone the same fate. The convents and the hospitals had suffered. The bishop's palace was entirely destroyed."[1] Captain John Knox also tells us that the château was considerably damaged in the siege.

On June 7th, 1762, General Murray wrote to the Right Honourable the Earl of Egremont, one of His Majesty's Secretaries of State: ". . . the King has two houses in Quebec, one in Upper Town stiled the Castle of St. Lewis, formerly the Governor-General's residence, so tattered by the effect of our artillery that I have been obliged to hire a home for myself. . . ."[2]

Had the English invasion broken the charm that had protected the Château St. Louis?—Perhaps not. It might easily have been razed to the ground in the siege. There it stood, French in all its appointments, but now by the fortunes of war it belonged to the British. And so they ran up the Union Jack of Queen Anne above its grey roofs!

[1]Dr. William Kingsford, *History of Canada, Vol. IV*.

[2]P. G. Roy, *Bulletin des Recherches Historiques* (Jan. 1909. Vol. XV, No. 1).

No more would the latest news from Paris and Versailles be discussed within the halls of the Château St. Louis; no more would be told the wild tales of the *coureurs des bois* and the pathetic accounts of the suffering missionaries. The new régime would have its own news—but from London—its own wonderful tales of conquests and expansion. . . .

Very soon after the capitulation, an opportunity presented itself for the French people of Canada to show their satisfaction with their new régime. On October 25th, 1760, George II of England died. The citizens of Montreal voluntarily adopted mourning for the prescribed period, and formed a committee who presented to Governor Gage of that city an address in which they assured him how much they appreciated the peace and prosperity that the British had brought to replace the privations and dangers they had heretofore suffered; that they "would never cease to exalt the mildness and moderation of their new masters" and, further, that "the favors will be forever engraven in our hearts in indelible characters".

In 1762 General Gage wrote the British Secretary of State: "His language" (referring to the French-Canadian) "is deserving of preservation, and is important, as it plainly shews the spirit in which the government was conducted. No invasion of their property, or insult to their persons, have gone unpunished. All reproaches to their subjection to the fate of arms, reviling on their customs or country, and all reflections on their religion, have been discountenanced and forbid. No distinction has been made betwixt the Briton and Canadian, but equally regarded as subjects of the same Prince. The soldiers live peaceably with the inhabitants, and they reciprocally acquire an affection for each other."

Twenty-five years later, the break between French Canada and France was almost complete. The French revolution sundered irrevocably the few ties remaining that had bound them together. The French-Canadian no longer understood the conduct of his own people, neither could he condone it. France had become godless—French Canada never would.

****

After following the fortunes of the French in Canada from 1620 up to the fall of Quebec in 1759, and the Treaty of Paris in 1763, one is curious to know what Canada was like in the early days of British rule—more especially what life was like in Quebec immediately after 1763.

In 1769 there was published in England a delightful, refreshing book called *The History of Emily Montague.*[3] This book is but a series of letters exchanged by a family and their friends in Canada with friends and relatives in England during the early days of the British in Canada. Excerpts from this lovely book form a colourful (though somewhat stern) picture of Quebec and the surrounding districts. It seems that, to the English, the weather, in particular the winter, was the dominating factor in their lives:

> "The savages assure us, my dear, on the information of the beavers, that we shall have a very mild winter; it seems, these creatures have laid in less winter stock than usual. I take it very ill, Lucy, that the beavers have better intelligence than we have . . . .
>
> "With submission to the beavers, the weather is very cold, and we have had a great deal of snow already; but they tell me 'tis nothing to what we shall have: they are taking precautions which make me shudder beforehand, pasting up the windows, and not leaving an avenue where cold can enter. . . .
>
> "The snow is six feet deep, so that we may be said to walk on our heads; that is, speaking *en philosophe*, we occupy the space we should have done in summer . . . our heels are now where our heads should be. . . .
>
> "I will never take a beaver's word again as long as I live: there is no supporting this cold; the Canadians say it is seventeen years since there has been so severe a season. I thought beavers had been people of more honor. . . .
>
> "We have had five days, the severity of which none of the natives remember to have ever seen equalled: 'tis said, the cold

[3]The Dictionary of Canadian Biography states: "Frances Brooke, née Moore, (1745-1789) novelist, was born in England 1745. She was the wife of the Reverend John Brooke, rector of Colney, in Norfolk, and afterwards (circa 1760-1768) garrison chaplain at Quebec. She joined her husband in Quebec about 1764, and while in Canada wrote what may be described as the first Canadian novel, *The History of Emily Montague*. (4 Vols. London, 1769). She returned to England in 1768 and died in 1789."

Property of L. G. Prevost, Esq., K.C.

ONE OF THE ROOMS IN
THE CHÂTEAU FRONTENAC

DECORATED BY MRS. HAYTER REED, 1920

Property of L. G. Prevost, Esq., K.C.

CHÂTEAU FRONTENAC, 1908-1909

MARIA CARLETON

—AFTER ROMNEY, 1787

Public Archives of Canada

Canadian Pacific Railway Co.

KENT HOUSE, MONTMORENCY FALLS

Property of L. G. Prevost, Esq., K.C.

CHÂTEAU FRONTENAC, 1908,
FROM LAVAL UNIVERSITY

MILITARY GUARD AT
CHÂTEAU FRONTENAC DURING
QUEBEC CONFERENCE, 1943

Canadian Pacific Railway Co.

National Film Board

QUEBEC CONFERENCE, 1943.
WINSTON CHURCHILL AND MACKENZIE
KING ARRIVING AT CHÂTEAU FRONTENAC

Canadian Pacific Railway Co.

A MODERN VIEW OF THE CHÂTEAU FRONTENA

is beyond all the thermometers here, tho' intended for the climate. The strongest wine freezes in a room which has a stove in it; even brandy is thickened to the consistence of oil; the largest wood fire, in a wide chimney, does not throw out its heat a quarter of a yard . . . we must be jovial or the blood will freeze in our veins . . . .

"I no longer wonder the elegant arts are unknown here; the rigour of the climate suspends the very powers of the understanding; what then must become of the imagination? . . . Genius will never mount high where the faculties of the mind are benumbed half the year."

One cannot help but smile on reading these lines. Though the winters are, at times, still as severe in Canada as they were in those early days, the Canadians have learned through years of trial how to combat that cold. They no longer huddle about "a wood fire in a wide chimney" and expect to keep warm. The houses are now centrally heated, and carefully insulated. Windows are not "pasted up" to keep out drafts; double windows, attached on the inner side at the first hint of winter, keep the warmth within. The glorious powdery snow is eagerly awaited by the Québecois in anticipation of skiing—a sport unknown in Emily Montague's day. Needless to say, these hospitable people have learned, too, to take care of their wine so that it does not freeze; and one has only to live in Quebec a few weeks to discover that the "elegant arts", the "powers of the understanding", the "imagination", the "faculties of the mind", are as lively here as anywhere in the world.

The English spent their leisure hours in much the same manner as their French neighbours—"Playing at cards"—"playing at shuttlecock"—"playing the fool"—"playing at love"—"driving in the open carriole or the covered-sleigh-with-curtains" — "dancing" — "skating"—"much hospitality" so says Emile Montague. There were picnics in the summer, and berry-picking expeditions; with trips by carriage or sleigh to the fascinating Montmorency Falls, which had steps of natural rock above them.[4]

Life in the little walled city was made more social and intim-

[4]These steps have long since been submerged by the backing up of the waters of the St. Lawrence River.

ate by the appearance on June 21st, 1764, of the first issue of a newspaper—the first in Quebec—*The Quebec Gazette.* It consisted of four sheets, with news in both French and English. Its subscription list consisted of a hundred and fifty persons. This paper is known today as the *Chronicle-Telegraph.* Printed now in English only, it is Quebec's only English newspaper.

Sir Guy Carleton[5] arrived in Canada for the second time, now as Administrator, on September 22nd, 1766. On his first visit he had taken an active and praiseworthy part in the battle of Quebec, during which he had been seriously wounded. Born in County Down in Ireland, Carleton brought all the rich understanding, the warm-heartedness, and the quick temper of the Irish to the government of Canada. Thirty-five years of his life were given to this country. His honest endeavours to unify the races in Canada were particularly worthy of him; he was ceaseless in his efforts to make them understand each other.

Sir Guy went to great pains to draw up plans for the citadel of Quebec, which was to be the centre for the military force. The present citadel, its bastion rising majestically and watchfully from the highest point of the rock above the city, the only thing in Quebec that can claim to "look down" on the Château Frontenac, is the successor to Carleton's original structure. In a letter to his government the Governor describes Quebec: "Its front is fortified by a bastioned rampart faced with masonry, built for the most part upon a rock without ditch or outworks; its profile slight for a fortress though substantial for an encampment, for ten or twelve battalions; its parapet is in very bad order."

In 1770 Carleton went to England for the purpose of advising the British Government regarding the drawing up of a new constitution for Canada. The result of his labours was the cherished (particularly by French-Canadians) Quebec Act of 1774, which righted many wrongs in the British administration of Canada and served to stem the subversive and rebellious currents that threatened to destroy any understanding between the English and French in Canada.

[5]Carleton was Administrator of the Province of Quebec (Canada) from September 24th, 1766, to October 26th, 1768, on which latter date he became Governor-in-Chief.

While in England on this occasion, Sir Guy courted and won the affection and the hand of Lady Maria Howard, daughter of the Earl of Effingham. He had hoped to marry her sister Anne, but on his return from Canada found that she was in love with someone else. When he returned to Canada for the third time in 1774, he brought his wife and their two young children with him.

Her early schooling in France had equipped Lady Carleton with an excellent knowledge of the language and an understanding of the French people, and upon her arrival in Canada she quickly won a special place in their hearts. She was a small, fair, dainty person and had a delightful personality. Some considered her haughty, but perhaps it was her quiet reserve, her erect carriage, her exquisite dignity, which gave that impression. She made friends slowly but they lasted her lifetime.

In 1775-76 the War of American Independence racked the English colonies south of Canada, and out of the travail, in the year 1776, was born a new nation, the United States of America.

Such an upheaval could not occur without creating considerable disturbance in Canada. From the beginning, General George Washington urged the French in Canada to join in the democratic movement against imperialism, to become eventually a part of the great republic. In a letter addressed to "The Inhabitants of Canada", he wrote:

> Friends and Brethren,
>
> The unnatural contest between the English colonies and Great Britain has now risen to such a height that arms alone must decide it. The colonies, confiding in the justice of their cause, and the purity of their intention, have reluctantly appealed to that Being in whose hands are all human events . . . Above all, we rejoice that our enemies have been deceived with regard to you. They have persuaded themselves, they have even dared to say, that the Canadians were not capable of distinguishing between the blessings of liberty and the wretchedness of slavery . . . . but they have been deceived; instead of finding in you a poverty of soul and baseness of spirit, they see with a chagrin, equal to our joy, that you are enlightened, generous, and virtuous; that you will not renounce your own rights, or serve as instruments to deprive

> your fellow-subjects of theirs. Come then, my brethren, unite with us in an indissoluble union, let us run together to the same goal . . . . Come then, ye generous citizens, range yourselves under the standard of general liberty, against which all the force and artifices of tyranny will never be able to prevail.
>
> George Washington.

Once again the French were tested in their allegiance to Great Britain, but the lure of the proposition to become the fourteenth state in an American democracy was not attractive enough to draw the French-Canadians from the protection of an English monarchy.

Two great American generals, Benedict Arnold and Richard Montgomery, gathered a large force and attacked Quebec in the winter of 1775. Every other point in Canada had given way before the American armies. The siege of Quebec was waged in bitter winter weather, and Montgomery, instead of "eating Christmas dinner in Quebec" as he had threatened, lay outside the walls of Quebec, a frozen corpse. Arnold was so badly wounded as to be incapacitated until spring, when the arrival of the English fleet brought about a speedy lifting of the siege.

Mr. James Thompson, the indefatigable diarist, has left us a most interesting account of the burial of General Montgomery. Mr. J. M. Le Moine quotes passages of this journal in his book, *Quebec, Past and Present,* from which the following is taken:

> "General Carleton, the then Governor-General, being satisfied as to his (Montgomery's) identity, ordered that the body should be decently buried, in the most private manner, and His Excellency entrusted the business to me. I accordingly had the body conveyed to a small log house in St. Louis street, the second from the corner of Ste. Ursule Street, owned by one François Gaubert, a cooper; and I ordered Henry Dunn, a joiner, to prepare a suitable coffin; this he complied with, having covered it with fine black cloth and lined it with flannel; I gave him no direction about the burying party, as I had a party of my soldiers in waiting at the Château to carry the corpse to the grave at the moment that General Carleton conceived proper. I next proceeded to Gaubert's, where I am told that

Mr. Dunn had just taken away the corpse; this was about the setting of the sun on the fourth of January, 1776. I accordingly stepped up to the place where I had ordered the grave to be dug (just alongside that of my first wife, within and near the surrounding wall of the powder magazine, in the gorge of the St. Louis Bastion), and found, in addition to the six men and Dunn, the undertaker, that the Rev. Dr. De Montmollin, the military chaplain, was in attendance. On satisfying myself that the grave was properly covered up, I went and reported the circumstances to General Carleton . . . I took care to mark the spot where Montgomery was buried . . . by having a small cut stone inserted in the pavement within the barrack square, and this precaution enabled me afterwards to point out the place to a nephew of the General, Mr. Lewis, who, hearing that the person who had the direction of the burial of his uncle's corpse was still living, came to Quebec, about the year 1818, to take away the remains. I repaired thither with young Mr. Lewis and several officers of the garrison, together with Chief Justice Sewell and some friends of the deceased. They accordingly took up the pavement, exactly in the direction of the grave. The skeleton was found complete, and when removed, a musket ball fell from the skull; the coffin was nearly decayed. No part of the black cloth of the outside, nor of the flannel of the inside was visible; a leather thong with which the hair had been tied was still in a state of preservation after a lapse of forty-three years. There is a spring of water near the place, which may have had the effect of hastening the decay of the contents of the grave."

Montgomery and Carleton had once been friends and neighbours in Ulster, but time and its endless paradoxes had decreed that they would each regard the other as a traitor and a tyrant. It is good to know that he who vanquished the other was of so fine a calibre as to see, personally, that the funeral of his enemy was fitting, and that, so the story goes, he took care to have his watch duly returned to the widow.

As the storm subsided, prosperity came to French Canada with expanded trade. There was no longer a scarcity of anything in Quebec or the other towns of Canada. In official circles, gaiety, hospitality and society held sway, and in Quebec the centre was the vice-regal court of old England in the "Castle of St. Lewis".

The year after Montgomery's repulse, the anniversary of Quebec's victory was celebrated in the Castle by a dinner given by the Governor and his Lady for sixty guests. It was followed by a public fête and a ball in the grand manner of England, and once again the lively music of court dances echoed in the halls of the mellow old building, reminiscent of such functions as that given by the Marquis de Tracy in 1667, before he returned to France.

****

Chapter Nine

SIR GUY CARLETON resigned as governor and left Canada in 1777. (He was to come again as Governor and as Lord Dorchester in 1784.) He was succeeded by a notable gentleman of Swiss-French extraction who had already a distinguished record, having won praise for himself at the battle of Ticonderoga in 1758, had commanded at Fort Edward and later rebuilt Fort Oswego. He had been Governor of Montreal from 1763 to 1766, and from 1766 to 1773 had been placed in command of Florida. This was Sir Frederick Haldimand. He arrived in Quebec in June, 1778.

Sir Frederick was greeted with much warmth, and with high expectations that he would follow, with equal zeal, the plans drawn up by Sir Guy Carleton for making Canada into a coherent whole. He did not disappoint them. Throughout his governorship, he had only the welfare of the Canadian people—irrespective of race—at heart.

Of outstanding note is Haldimand's management of the Loyalists who were settling in Upper Canada at a time when that section was a tinder-box of resentment and dissent. The tact with which he soothed the discord was a miracle of diplomacy. It is only necessary to this story, however, to say that had it not been for Sir Frederick Haldimand, Canada might not have been held in the British Empire—notwithstanding the result of the Battle of the Plains of Abraham and the Treaty of Paris.

The first problem, and doubtless the greatest disturbance with which Governor Haldimand had to contend, was the infiltration of anti-British propaganda which was being subversively circulated throughout the province. Then, too, there were rumours that a further attempt might be made by France to retake Canada; and that other foreign powers might try to take her by force simply to curb England's sea-power, which had become so extensive with the acquisition of Canada. All of which added to the general unrest that filled the two peoples of Canada.

Carleton's early plans for a proper Citadel were closely followed by Haldimand when he undertook to erect it of stone. Even if the project received due consideration from England and if the necessary care were taken to send the right materials and tools, it was to be a work of many years. It did seem, at first, as if the Home Government of Canada's new ruler would be no more prone to develop her fortifications and resources than had been the former ruler of New France.

Although Sir Frederick Haldimand is described as an attractive person, with an excellent personality, possessing fine social instincts, as well as an appreciative eye for the ladies, he never married. He was "tall, well-built, with most agreeable manners . . . having fineness of face".[1] But perhaps he was too busy in his progressive military and political career to take any of his female acquaintances seriously.

The absence of a chatelaine in the Château St. Louis did not, by any means, deter its social life. There were countless gay functions during Haldimand's governorship. On January 18th, 1784, a brilliant ball and supper were held in the elegant ballroom of the Château St. Louis and all Quebec's élite gathered there to do honour to the Queen whose birthday it was. It is said[2] that that evening was Sunday, and in the more austere circles of the city it was considered due reproach from heaven that a heavy snowstorm and blizzard arose when the celebration was at its height, and felled the cross from the Cathedral. Be that as it may, the ball was a tremendous success, with dancing kept up until the small hours of morning. However, the French-English *Gazette* of January 22nd, 1784, said, regarding this event, "Sunday last, the 18th, being the anniversary of Her Majesty's birthday, on *Monday* noon a Royal Salute was fired from the Ramparts and three volleys from the troops on the Parade; and in the *evening* His Excellency the Governor gave a magnificent ball at the Château St. Lewis.[3]

A similar item covering the celebration in honour of the King's birthday appeared in the *Gazette* on June 10th, 1784.

The conscientious Governor did not neglect his administrative duties while society gathered about him nightly. He could never

[1]Jean McIlwraith, *Sir Frederick Haldimand.* (Makers of Canada Series).
[2]J. M. Le Moine.
[3]Anglicized spelling of St. Louis found in old documents, etc.

be accused of dilatoriness. No affair of State, no matter how insignificant, was overlooked, pushed aside, or treated lightly by Haldimand even though he was doubtless hard pressed at times. However, it may have been the extensive entertaining he did in the Château St. Louis that made Sir Frederick feel that this place where he resided, entertained, and conducted his business, was too small to serve all three purposes adequately. In any case, in 1784, he built a fine new house, very near to the Château St. Louis, which he furnished in the English manner and named the Château Haldimand. Its cornerstone was laid by him with due ceremony on May 5th, 1784.[4] When finished it was a grand place, though simple in outline and design; it served as offices for the Legislature, and at the same time had large rooms for public functions. (The first function of note to be held in the new Château was an elegant reception on January 19th, 1787, in honour of the birthday of Queen Charlotte of Mecklenburg, Consort of King George III[5]—though, of course, Sir Frederick was, by that time, no longer Governor and no longer in Quebec.)

Because he was so impressed with the natural beauty of Montmorency Falls—some seven or eight miles from Quebec—Sir Frederick built there a lovely house for his summer residence. One of his dear friends, the Baroness Riedesel, visited it and was charmed with both the house and the site chosen for it. The name of the house then was Haldimand House. Today, much changed and enlarged (until probably little of the original building is left), it bears the name Kent House because it was subsequently occupied (1791-1796) by the Duke of Kent, of whom later mention will be made in this chronicle.

It was the Baroness Riedesel who taught Sir Frederick how to make pickled cucumbers which he liked so well. "It was through him," writes the Baroness, "that the art—if such it may be called—became generally known in Canada."[6]

"He, (Haldimand) may be regarded as the very first man in Canada who introduced the love of gardening. He laid out the public gardens in Quebec. The handsome residence of Montmor-

[4]George Gale in *Historic Tales of Old Quebec.*
[5]J. M. Le Moine in *Picturesque Quebec.* (For footnote 6 see p. 100).

ency Falls, and the gardens, as they exist, were in the first instance his work."[7]

In 1780, five large cases of books arrived at the Château Haldimand, sent out from London by Richard Cumberland, the dramatist. These were to form the first library in Quebec and had been requested by the enterprising Governor Haldimand. These books finally came into the possession of the Literary and Historic Society of Quebec which was founded by Lord Dalhousie in 1824.

"The man who is a strong partisan will be defended by those of his own way of thinking unto the third and fourth generations, but he who tries to do justice to both sides is almost certain to be abused by both and their children's children. This has been Haldimand's fate and it rests with the disinterested student of history to search for the cause of his unpopularity. Undoubtedly he never sought public favour; to the King and his ministers he owed an account of his stewardship and them alone he sought to please. . . . His hardest task was not the repulsion of actual rebel attacks upon the frontiers, but the discovery and suppression of the subtle means employed to undermine the allegiance of the French Canadians." Thus writes Jean McIlwraith in a biography of Sir Frederick Haldimand.[8]

Documents and letters left among an assortment of personal papers speak for themselves of the "constant goodness and generous kindness" of this man who has been maligned by some with accusations of cruelty!

On November 16th, 1784, the British ship, *Atlanta*, weighed anchor at Quebec and set sail for England. His Excellency, Sir Frederick Haldimand, was on board. His task in Canada was finished. The people had bidden him "an affectionate and respectful adieu . . . the *Atlanta* returned the farewell gun salute and immediately set sail with a fair wind for England".[9] His task was over—but not the troubles he had brought upon himself in all innocence and in the belief that he had been doing his duty. The accusations of his enemies followed him to England and made him

[6] and [7]Dr. William Kingsford in *History of Canada,* Vol. I.
[8]Jean McIlwraith's *Sir Frederick Haldimand.*
[9]*The Gazette,* November 18th, 1784.

most unhappy. However, the spite was of no avail, for he was subsequently invested with the Order of the Bath by the King.

In his diary, Haldimand wrote proudly, "The King in handing me the ribbon, told me that he could not give it to any one with more pleasure, and when I kissed the King's hand he held it to me with affection."

Another excerpt from this diary is interesting: "Was at Court, which was very brilliant. I found Sir Guy Carleton there, and told him that when he should go to Canada he would find there my carriages, post chaise, and twelve horses, which would be much at his service. . . . I offered him the house at Montmorency but he said Lady Carleton would not take it at any price on account of her children."

Sir Frederick died quietly, without too much pain from his everlastingly swollen ankles and knees, on June 5th, 1791, at Yverdun, Switzerland. No monument to this worthy gentleman has ever been erected in Canada, but in Westminster Abbey a simple bronze tablet bears the following inscription in French:

Du Chevalier Frederick Haldimand, Général et
Colonel d'un Regiment d'Infanterie au Service
de Sa Majesté; cy-devant Général Commandant
en Chef dans l'Amérique Septentrionale;
Gouverneur de la Province de Québec;
Inspecteur Général des Troupes dans les
Isles Occidentales, et Chevalier du très
honorable Ordre du Bain; installé
le 19me Jour de Mai MDCCLXXXVIII.

In Quebec City, a block away from the Château Frontenac, there is a short street on rising ground which is known as Haldimand Hill. It is paved with cobblestones, and is by no means a thoroughfare. It is the only reminder Quebec possesses of the good Sir Frederick Haldimand.

****

Sir Guy Carleton returned to Canada as Governor bearing the title of Lord Dorchester.[10]

[10]Governor-in-Chief of the Province of Quebec, Oct. 26, 1768 to June 27, 1778; Governor-in-Chief of the Province of Quebec, Oct. 23, 1786 to Dec. 25, 1791; Governor-in-Chief and Captain General of the British Provinces in North America, Dec. 26, 1791 to Dec. 15, 1796.
Left Quebec for the last time July 9, 1796.

In spite of the disfavour he had unwittingly incurred among the English in Canada during his previous term of office, he was as warmly welcomed by them as by the French, whose cause he had so zealously championed. He had resigned because of differences with the British Foreign Minister, Viscount Germain. It is not claimed that either was always in the right, and yet the reader is inclined to sympathize with Sir Guy when it is known that Sir Frederick Haldimand had at first refused his commission as Governor of Canada rather than work with Germain, and that at one time Germain had actually been cashiered for cowardice on the field of battle, and was generally distrusted.

It was during Lord Dorchester's second governorship that the Constitutional Act was passed in 1791, wherein the Province of Quebec was divided into two separate Provinces, to be called Upper Canada (Ontario) and Lower Canada (Quebec), and within each was set up a Legislative Council and an Assembly. Each province had its own Lieutenant-Governor, with the Governor-General (at that time Lord Dorchester) in authority over all.

There then ensued a half-century of representative government which terminated in hard-won responsible government.

A particularly bright social highlight of these years in the old city of Quebec was the visit of William Henry, Duke of Clarence, son of King George III.[11] At this time the Duke was a midshipman aboard the frigate *Pegasus*, and it is said that he enjoyed great popularity during his brief visit to Quebec when he visited Lord and Lady Dorchester in the Château St. Louis and was entertained at the usual functions held in the Château Haldimand.

By this time Lord Dorchester's health was beginning to fail. He was now seventy-two. On July 9th, 1796, to the great regret of all the Canadian people, he and Lady Maria left Canada. Lady Maria was still lively and charming, a gay little figure in tastefully bright gowns, carefully coiffured white hair, and high-heeled shoes. They retired to their estate at Kempshot, near Basingstoke, England. Their years of retirement were immensely saddened by the loss of six sons who were killed in quick succession on the battlefields of Europe. Through all her grief, it is said that milady

[11] J. M. Le Moine in *The Port of Quebec, 1535-1900*

carried herself with that superb dignity and bearing which made a never-to-be-forgotten impression upon all who were privileged to know her. Lord Dorchester died peacefully at Stubbings, near Maidenhead, on November 10th, 1808.

At Grey Wells Hill, near the old family estate at Kempshot, Basingstoke, the present Lord and Lady Dorchester reside. The title is not of direct descent but rather a royal restoration in 1899, in the person of the then last member of the family, through the courtesy of Queen Victoria. The present Lord Dorchester, a tall, slim, erect gentleman who claims he is "getting on in years", is the grandson of the descendant for whom the Queen revived the title.[12] He succeeded to the title in 1925.

Many reminders of the first Lord Dorchester's years in Canada are preserved on this graceful old estate at Basingstoke. The old coach used by Sir Guy in Quebec is still there—a piece worthy of any museum; the elegant silver coffee-pot and tea-pot, over which Lady Carleton once presided so charmingly in the Château St. Louis, are there, too. Perhaps Lord Dorchester could be persuaded that Canada, or more particularly Quebec, would be a fitting place for the final repose of these heirlooms.

The title will again become extinct since Lord Dorchester's two children are both daughters. On a recent visit to Canada, during which Lord and Lady Dorchester visited Quebec and made the Château Frontenac their home, Lord Dorchester remarked, "I've been all over the world and there's nothing to compare with Quebec anywhere. . . ."[13]

[12] and [13]Lord Dorchester so advised the author in Quebec in 1947.

Chapter Ten

HIS ROYAL HIGHNESS Edward Augustus, fourth son of King George III, later Duke of Kent and Strathern, came to Quebec in August, 1791,[1] when he was twenty-four years old. He was Colonel of the Regiment of the Seventh Royal Fusiliers who were then being stationed in Quebec.

Beginning with a brilliant *levée* in his honour at the Château St. Louis, the four years of the Prince's stay in Quebec were among the liveliest and brightest in all the history of the city. He was enormously popular, the centre of the social life of the city. The young ladies of Quebec, as well as those of Montreal, vied with each other in their efforts to win the royal favour.

Although the Duke of Kent (as the Prince is usually known to Canadian history) was gallant and gracious to all the ladies, his heart was held by the charming Alphonsine Thérèse Bernardine Julie de Montgenet de St. Laurent, Baronne de Fortisson, who had followed him to Quebec. They were inseparable for twenty-seven years but they never married. The Baroness was a Roman Catholic; the Duke was the son of a ruling King of England, in direct line for the throne and might conceivably someday be *head of the Church of England*. Such a marriage was, therefore, forbidden by the Royal Marriage Act of 1688. There was some talk of a morganatic marriage[2] but there is no irrefutable evidence to support this rumour. Mr. Hector Bolitho, in his biography *Queen Victoria*, mentions that children were born of this union.

Many ill-starred romances have happy endings. This one did not. In spite of having lived openly together at Kent House (Haldimand's House at Montmorency Falls), and at his winter quarters on St. Louis street (No. 25 St. Louis street—since then also known as Kent House), and constantly creating a furore

[1]J. M. Le Moine in *The Port of Quebec, 1535-1900,* gives the date of the Prince's arrival in Quebec as August 18th, 1791.

[2]Mr. Edgar Andrew Collard's article in the column, *All Our Yesterdays,* in *The Gazette,* Montreal, April 14th, 1947.

among the social leaders of the city as to whether *La Baronne* should be invited whenever His Royal Highness was to be present, this devoted couple were still aware of the duties which impinged upon the Prince as a scion of the Royal Family of England. Nevertheless, when the Duke left Canada for duty in the West Indies in January, 1794, Madame de St. Laurent, Baronne de Fortisson, accompanied him. Some years later they returned to Canada and lived for a time in Halifax where the Duke was stationed. But eventually the day came when England bade the Prince return to the fold, to marry and produce an heir to the throne. Like a dutiful son, the Prince said goodbye to his lady and sailed away from her forever. History does not divulge that they ever met again.

Prince Edward, Duke of Kent, duly married Princess Victoria of Saxe-Coburg-Leiningen, and the result of this imperially-arranged union was a daughter who was destined to become the greatest woman ruler of all time—Victoria.

Meanwhile, in far-away Quebec, to which she had returned, the Baronne de Fortisson lived out her days alone at Kent House on the beautiful Falls, and though surrounded by friends, many of whom had been personal friends of His Royal Highness, she remained in dignified retirement emerging only on rare occasions.[3]

There is still in existence a commemorative bit of poetry[4] which is most expressive of the Duke's popularity in Canada:

How he looked when he danced, when he sat at his ease,
When His Highness had sneezed or was going to sneeze. . . .
They have stolen his gloves, and purloined his cravat,
Even scraped a souvenir from the nap of his hat. . . .

In the shadow of the Château Frontenac there is an old house, simple and severe in design, repeatedly restored and considerably altered since 1794, now in use as business offices, which was once the headquarters of the Duke of Kent during the winters of his stay in Quebec. This, too, is Kent House. Some legends have it that it had originally been built by the infamous Intendant Bigot (1748-1759) for one of his mistresses, Madame de Pean, formerly Angelique des Meloises, the wicked beauty of Kirby's novel, *The*

[3]Some reports say that she retired to a convent in 1818.
[4]Thanks to J. M. Le Moine who has recorded it in *Maple Leaves,* (1863).

Golden Dog. However, in refutation of this, a small bronze plaque now affixed to the wall of this building reads:

Kent House
D'Ailleboust, Governor of
New France, occupied this
House in 1648.
De Ramezay here signed the
capitulation of Quebec in 1759.
The Duke of Kent,
Father of Queen Victoria,
resided here from 1792 to 1794.

Bigot came to Quebec one hundred years after d'Ailleboust occupied it while the Château St. Louis was being repaired. Therefore, Bigot could not have built it; possibly he purchased it—or more probably appropriated it—for his paramour.

****

In the summer of 1796, Isaac Weld, Jr., visited Canada. Three years afterwards his book, *Travels into North America*, was published in London. The descriptions of Quebec in this book are wonderfully interesting to anyone who would know what Canada was like in those early days.

"The Upper Town," writes Weld, speaking of the city, "is extremely agreeable . . . the air is as pure as possible and the inhabitants are never oppressed with heat in summer." Mr. Weld explains that the city was far from being well laid out, the streets being narrow and very irregular. His description of the Château is scarcely romantic or glamorous: ". . . a plain building of common stone, situated in an open place . . . stands just on the verge of an inaccessible part of the rock; behind it, on the outside, there is a long gallery, from whence, if a pebble were let drop, it would fall at least sixty feet perpendicularly . . . the chateau is built without any regularity of design. . . It is not a place of strength." Weld does, however, represent Quebec's social life as being bright and merry. The Regiments paraded regularly in Place d'Armes during fine weather, and the cream of society disported itself of a summer evening upon the lawns of the garden on the other side of the Château and listened leisurely to a band concert.

Prosperity seemed now a general state of affairs, with plenty of food on the market at moderate prices. Since the country was not yet manufacturing to any extent, the imports were numerous, consisting of household goods and drugs, leather and iron goods, clothing, wines and spirits, tropical fruits and spices, etc. Exports were a thriving source of revenue—furs, wheat, flour, timber, ginseng, flaxseed, and so forth, were regularly sent to England. By the year 1805, the public accounts of Quebec showed the revenue from civil sources to be £33,633 currency, and the expenditures, £33,003. The number of vessels arriving in the port of Quebec was 146, a total tonnage of 25,136.

The loveliness of the scenery of Quebec seems to have been a source of delight to everyone who has ever visited the vicinity. Weld, a great world traveller, wrote that its beauty, diversity and grandeur surpassed anything he had seen in America, "or indeed in any other part of the globe. It is scarcely possible for the imagination to paint to itself anything more sublime." To those who have seen Quebec in all her summer greenness and radiance, or in the frosty delicacy of her winter snows, Weld's words do not seem exaggerated—only quite, quite true, and richly deserved.

Winter in Canada in the late seventeen hundreds was a vastly different season (discounting the weather) than it now is. "By means of carioles or sledges, the Canadians transport themselves over the snow from place to place, in the most agreeable manner, and with a degree of swiftness that appears almost incredible," writes Mr. Weld. Today, sleighdriving is no longer a necessary method of transportation but a gentle sport to be indulged in when one wishes to move at a more languid pace . . . and yet Quebec would hardly be Quebec, even today, without its carioles . . . or its calèches in summer.

The turn of the century found Canadian affairs at a fairly even tenor, and the year 1801 passed uneventfully, peacefully, prosperously. The new constitution was fitfully seized with growing pains, but that was scarcely more than was to be expected. Lord Dorchester was keenly missed by both French and English. He had brought to Quebec a bit of England for the English; for the French a traditional brilliance reminiscent of the old days; a ready hand and a patient ear for those less fortunate of both races; a graciousness towards high and low; and, of even greater value, an open mind on Canada's complex problems and a broad understanding of the conditions that existed in this adolescent country.

Major General Robert Prescott, who was left in charge of the government on Dorchester's departure, was a good, kindly and honourable gentleman who soon became very popular with the majority of the people. His dealings with the government, however, were fraught with misunderstanding on both sides, and it was not long before matters came to the point where the breach between administrator and legislature was almost as wide as before Dorchester's arrival. Briefly, the trouble hinged upon the Executive Council's questioning of Prescott's right to make certain dispositions of the Crown Lands. The upset eventually reached the Home Government and, as Prescott had previously requested that he be recalled, he was duly summoned home, and left Canada on July 5th, 1799.

✥✥✥✥✥✥✥✥✥✥✥

Of all the books that have been written dealing with the brilliant and lavish quasi-regal court of Quebec at the close of the eighteenth century, none are more excitingly written than those of Sir James McPherson Le Moine. In particular, his *Maple Leaves* are outstanding in narration of social affairs of the city of Quebec in those days. He describes a ball held in the Château by His Excellency Governor Prescott for the presentation of members of society to Mrs. Prescott. "In the imitation of a Royal apartment" writes Sir James, "to prevent the possibility of anyone being caught sitting, every chair and seat of every description had been carefully removed. . . At length the General and his lady,[5] attended by the Aide-de-Camp, the Deputy Adjutant-General, Deputy Quarter-Master General, etc., and a number of other officers on the staff, made their *entrée*, and being led up to the Captain General each lady made a very low curtsy, her knees almost touching the carpet, and regained an erect posture. Immediately on rising, His Excellency kissed her, and although eighty winters at least had passed

[5]This excerpt is a quotation used by J. M. Le Moine which, as he says, is taken from the journal of a certain Lieutenant Landman of the Royal Engineers who was stationed in Quebec at that time.

their chills through his blood, it was remarked that he performed that agreeable part of his official duties with the warmth of his most youthful days. Each individual was in like manner presented to Mrs. Prescott. All the ladies and gentlemen thus newly admitted into the aristocratic sphere, moved into the ballroom as quickly as each presentation had been completed, after which (all being in the ballroom) a flourish of trumpets was sounded in the orchestra as two doors at the opposite extremity of the room opened announcing that the King and Queen, represented by the Governor and his lady, preceded by the master of ceremonies, and followed by his numerous staff, entered by the door on his right, and the Queen, (Mrs. Prescott), attended by her daughter, Mrs. Baldwin, and by four or five other ladies, in some way either connected with the Governor's family or with the principal officers of the Government, entered by the doors on the left. . . . The band struck up 'God Save The King' . . . and the King and Queen walked around the room."

Lieutenant Landman, from whose journal the foregoing is taken by Sir James Le Moine, continues to write of the society of Quebec and the fashions of the period. "This lady was of large proportions, about sixty years of age, dressed in the extreme of fashion forty years gone by, her hair frizzed up a yard high above her head, increasing in width as it rose in height, the whole well-covered with marechal and pink powder, with some decorations of lace and ribbons scattered about the top, and surmounted by a splendid plume of ostrich feathers. Her body was encased in a long and stiff pair of stays, displaying an elegantly carved and ornamented bust, and leaving the neck and bosom uncovered, an immense pair of hoops spread out her dress to the extent of a yard at least on each side, so as to cover the entire length of the sofa upon which she was seated quite erect. Her sleeves just covered her elbows and were profusely trimmed with rich lace; from her ears depended a mass of gold and valuable stones; round her neck were four or five necklaces of coral, of amber, of pearls, of beads of various colours and some gold chains; but there was one in particular, larger than all the rest, and hanging so low as to require being supported from falling on her lap by a large clasp or hook fastened to the centre of the lap of her dress—this caused the said chain to hang in two festoons, upon each of which were fastened four family miniatures of the largest dimensions, and round each arm, which was left quite uncovered, there were three similar portraits, together with sundry other bracelets; her fingers were plentifully supplied with rings, and she had one on each thumb. But the watch formed not only the most conspicuous, but also the most costly of all the ornaments, being set with diamonds and fastened to her side by a large flowered hook, from which some ten or twelve short chains were suspended, each finished with a swivel holding a large seal or a key of the diameter of a half-crown, a scent-bottle, a gentleman's mourning ring, or other trinkets of the like description. I cannot close this already too lengthy detail of the dress of the very celebrated Mrs. S . . . t of Royal ancestry, without adverting to the pink stockings, short dress, and white satin shoes, having heels two or three inches high, neatly covered with red morocco leather, and fastened by a handsome pair of buckles, containing many brilliant stones."[6]

Before the arrival, on October 18th, 1807, of the newly-appointed Governor, Lieutenant-General Sir Henry James Craig, the government passed into the hands, consecutively, of Sir Robert Shore Milnes, and the Honourable Thomas Dunn, senior Executive Councillor.

Sir Robert Milnes took the reins on July 31st, 1799. The best that can be said of this administrator is that he did as well as he knew how to do but that it proved too mediocre. In October of 1804 he sought leave of absence on account of ill health. He was suffering from recurrent attacks of a "severe bilious fever he had contracted in the West Indies."[7] It was not until the following August that he finally set sail for England, leaving the government in the hands of Mr. Dunn. It may be said of Milnes that, during his somewhat lengthy term as administrator, he was well liked by the few who knew him personally, but for the masses his office lacked the pomp and ceremony with which wealth and rank had heretofore endowed government house and all its functions. Milnes was

[6]Excerpts from Lieutenant Landman's journal, taken from J. M. Le Moine's *Maple Leaves,* (1906).

[7]Dr. William Kingsford's *History of Canada, Vol. VII.*

obviously extremely poor. No brilliant balls or soirées marked his passing across the Quebec stage.

Matters moved quite smoothly for Mr. Dunn during the two years he was in charge of the government. In fact, it appears that whenever a governor left Canada, the interim, until the new governor's arrival, was usually, and capably, filled by the estimable Mr. Dunn. He was always on hand when most needed.

Sir James H. Craig arrived in *H.M.* frigate, *Horatio*. He was a Scotsman and in every respect a most worthy gentleman—but, unfortunately, the wrong man for Canada at this particular time. Extremely dignified, a strict disciplinarian, a firm believer in class distinction, very, very British—so much so that he had little patience with, and less understanding of, the French in Canada than any governor before him. He was somehow under the impression that the members of the Legislature of Quebec were but a group of ill-trained, uneducated men who could certainly do no less than precipitate affairs of state into chaos. As soon as he undertook to "train them in the way they should go"—that is, the way he considered they should go—he was met by bitter and sarcastic opposition which served only to set the French and English more fiercely against each other. There was the occasion on which he summarily dissolved the House on the grounds that the members were wasting their time! A Caesarean move that set all parties against him.

The Seventh Parliamentary session of Quebec's Legislature opened on December 10th, 1810. Among the list of appropriations for which bills were duly passed, we find,

"£14,980 for repairs to the Castle of St. Louis".

Governor Craig had begun remodelling the Château St. Louis in 1808. He had it enlarged and a third story added which greatly improved its appearance and provided more space—something that had been badly needed for many years—something that Sir Frederick Haldimand could have had done had he not preferred to build the Château Haldimand. In 1808 the repairs, which Craig was then considering, had been estimated to cost possibly £7,000, but, as evidenced by the item of appropriation in December, 1810, it had cost more than double that amount.

From the time Governor Craig re-occupied the restored

Château St. Louis, that building became known as the "new Château", and the Château Haldimand was dubbed the "old Château".

An excellent description of the Château St. Louis in the years 1806-7-8 has been left for us by John Lambert:[8]

"The old château, or castle of St. Louis, is built upon the verge of an inaccessible part of the rock, and separated by a court-yard from the new building which fronts the parade. . . It was formerly occupied by the Governor for his residence; but on the erection of the other, was converted into public offices. It is now undergoing considerable improvements for the use of Sir James Craig. It is to be raised one story higher, and the expenses are to be defrayed by the colony, agreeable to an act passed for that purpose by the Provincial Parliament. When finished it will possess every requisite for the abode of the most distinguished person in the colony. Its situation, for fine prospects, and extensive views of the river and surrounding country cannot be surpassed in any part of the Upper Town. Behind the building is a large stone gallery or balcony, even with the lower apartments. This gallery, which serves as a very agreeable promenade, is situated more than two hundred and fifty feet above the level of the river and commands a beautiful panorama of the Lower Town, etc. . . To complete the plan upon which the old château (St. Louis) is rebuilding, the guardhouse on the right has been pulled down, and a new one of stone is constructing on a larger scale. The back of this building and the sides, which will open into the court-yard, are to contain the Governor's horses and carriages, and a part is to be appropriated for a riding school. The other château on the left (Haldimand), it is said, is also coming down in part, for the purpose of making both wings uniform and enlarging the entrance to the grand château."

Since Governor Craig considered himself above making any conciliatory moves towards the political parties of his government, which would have ameliorated a difficult state of affairs, he became even more peevish and highhanded than ever. As in the case of many of his predecessors, ill health can be justly blamed for many of the tactless things he said and did. He was sixty and had dropsy.

[8]John Lambert, *Travels Through Lower Canada and the United States of America in the Years 1806-1807-1808,* (1810).

Added to this, Canada—or more precisely, conditions in Quebec—proved a little too much for him. After four years of it, he left for England.

By his pompous ways, the Governor had earned himself the dubious nickname of "Little King Craig". And as he sailed away from Canada on *H.M.S. Amelia*, on June 19th, 1811, Craig was suffering not only from dropsy and other infirmities, but also from a bitter frame of mind towards mankind in general—Canadians in particular. On the voyage home, his physical condition grew rapidly worse, and it was feared he would not live to reach England. He did—but died seven months later.

Once again Mr. Dunn came nobly forward and filled the breach until the arrival on September 14th, 1811, of Sir George Prevost, the new Governor.

****

In so far as was still possible under ever-changing conditions, Sir George Prevost followed the lines of conduct in government affairs which Lord Dorchester had found so successful. Having proved himself in civil affairs while Lieutenant-Governor of Nova Scotia, Prevost set himself to heal the wounds that Craig had inflicted. He spoke French naturally and was thus so far established in the good graces of the French-Canadians, which may be said to have set him off to a good start.

Had the world—especially this continent—remained at peace, there is little doubt that Prevost's governorship would have been very successful. But now there was to be war between Great Britain and America.

The grounds for war were found in certain British Orders-in-Council which the United States claimed were having a damaging effect on their trade. The origin of these Orders-in-Council was indirectly due to Napoleon. In 1806, Napoleon, in an attempt to ruin England, had issued his "Berlin Decrees" which placed England under blockade. Neutral ships were forbidden to enter English ports, and all use of her manufactures was banned on the European continent. England's Navy, however, rendered these decrees ineffectual, but in retaliation England issued Orders-in-Council forbidding all nations to trade with France. Her Navy was well able to enforce these Orders. The result was considerable impairment of American trade with France. The United States objected.

At the same time, certain correspondence between Governor Craig of Canada and his emissary to Boston, Captain John Henry, on the matter of persuading New England to leave the union of the States, reached the hands of President Madison. Captain Henry, in a fit of anger against Craig for not rendering him sufficient remuneration for his services, had sold the letter to the President of the United States.

Although England was, at this point, intimating her withdrawal of the offensive Orders-in-Council, the cry in the United States was that Britain "had tempted the fidelity of New England". On June 18th, 1812, the Congress of the United States passed an Act enabling the President to declare war on Great Britain. On June 19th, Madison exercised his new powers and declared war. On June 23rd, the Orders-in-Council were speedily withdrawn.[9]

It soon became obvious that the American idea of waging war on Great Britain was to attack Canada. After all, was it not the Governor of Canada who had tampered with the fidelity of one of the States? The Americans also considered that the French in Canada must have received, by this time, brimming measure of rule by England and would, with a little encouragement, be ready to rise against her. This time the Americans were even more ill-advised than they had been in 1775. Whereas, in the war of 1775, the majority of French-Canadians had remained neutral, this time they sprang readily to arms beside their English countrymen and together they presented a united front to the United States.

As far as this tale is concerned, the War of 1812-14 was confined to Upper Canada (Ontario). The Lower province suffered only skirmishes, although orders came thick and fast from the "Castle of St. Lewis" on the cliffs of Quebec, directing various military proceedings.

While Canada was involved in a threatening war from such close quarters—a war that was not actually of her own making—England was struggling to overthrow Napoleon on the continent of the Old World. By 1814 this war drew to a close; the dictator

[9]Charles G. D. Roberts, *History of Canada.*

was finally consigned to the Island of Elba, and the British troops thereby released from action in Europe, swarmed across the Atlantic to Canada's aid. Slowly the American battalions were driven out of Canada and pursued deep into their own territory.

In an engagement near Plattsburgh, during the last year of the war, Governor Prevost, at the head of his troops, made an unscheduled retreat when faced with sure death—but glory—for himself and his men had they stood their ground, submitted to being surrounded by the enemy, and eventually made prisoners. Prevost had always displayed great personal bravery in action but, it now appeared, he lacked resolution in such an emergency as he faced at Plattsburgh. And because few military men in those days understood that a man, even a brave soldier, could shelve his pride and love of glory when the sacrifice of his men would avail nothing, he was subsequently subjected, upon his return to England in the spring of 1815, to the great indignity of being called to court martial to explain his unprecedented action.

Somehow one feels it was fortunate that Prevost died before he could appear at a court martial so damaging to his reputation. During the last months of the war his health had begun to give way. Upon his departure for England in April, 1815, he had chosen to sail from St. John, New Brunswick, and had unwisely made the long journey on foot, from Quebec to St. John, across uninhabited, snow-covered, frozen country. As a result his exhaustion was extreme and he was never himself again. He died on January 5th, 1816.

The stigma which was attached to Prevost's otherwise unblemished name and record was subsequently dispelled when the Prince Regent publicly declared his approbation of the distinguished services rendered the Crown by the late Sir George Prevost, and caused certain distinctive additions to be made to the Prevost coat-of-arms.

A little research will so often reveal that the incomprehensible acts of certain men in key positions are the result of their interpretation of orders given them by their superiors. In this case Lord Bathurst, Great Britain's Colonial Secretary, had issued the following instructions to Governor Prevost, during the war of 1812:

"You will take care not to expose His Majesty's troops to being cut off; and guard against whatever might commit the safety of the forces placed under your command."

****

At the session of Parliament which opened in January of 1815, a grant of £500 was made to one Joseph Bouchette, surveyor-general for the Province of Quebec, for a topographical map of the province. What is of even more pertinent interest to us is that, in the same year, Bouchette's book *Topography of Canada* was published. In this book, Bouchette writes at length on the Château St. Louis:

"Of these buildings the Castle of St. Louis, being the most prominent object on the summit of the rock will obtain the first notice: It is a handsome stone building, seated near the edge of a precipice, something more than two hundred feet high, and supported towards the steep by a solid work of masonry, rising nearly half the height of the edifice, and surmounted by a spacious gallery, from whence there is a most commanding prospect over the *bason,* the Isle d'Orleans, Point Levi, and the surrounding country. The whole pile is a hundred and sixty-two feet long by forty-five broad, and three stories high; but in the direction of the Cape it has the appearance of being much more lofty; each extremity is terminated by a small wing, giving to the whole an easy and regular character: the interior arrangement is convenient, the decorative part tasteful and splendid, suitable in every respect for the residence of the governor general. It was built shortly after the city was fortified with solid works, consequently had but little to recommend it to notice: for a long series of years it was neglected so much as to be suffered to go to decay, and ceasing to be the residence of the commander-in-chief, was used only for the offices of government until the year 1808 when a resolution passed the provincial parliament for repairing and beautifying it; the sum of £7,000 was at the same time voted, and the work forthwith commenced. The money supplied was inadequate to defray the expenses upon the grand scale the improvements were commenced, but an additional grant was made to cover the whole charge; and in the present day, as a residence for His Majesty's representative, it is highly creditable to the liberality and public spirit of the province.

"Sir James Craig was the first who took possession of it. The part properly called the Chateau occupies one side of the square or courtyard; on the opposite side stands an extensive building (Chateau Haldimand) divided among the various offices of government both civil and military, that are under the immediate control of the governor; it contains also a handsome suite of apartments, wherein the balls and other public entertainments of the court are always given. During the delapidated state of the Chateau (St. Louis) this building was occupied by the family of the governors.

"Both the exterior and interior are in very plain style (speaking of the Chateau Haldimand); it forms part of the curtain that ran between the two exterior bastions of the old fortress St. Louis; adjoining it are several other buildings of smaller size, appropriated to similar uses, a guard house, stables, and extensive riding house. The fortress of St. Louis covered about four acres of ground, and formed nearly a parallelogram; on the western side two strong bastions on each angle were connected by a curtain, in the centre of which was a sallyport; the other faces presented works of nearly a similar description, but of less dimensions. . . . On the south-west side of the Chateau there is a most excellent and well-stocked garden, one hundred and eighty yards long, and seventy broad; and on the opposite side of the Rue de Carrieres there is another, one hundred and seventy yards long by eighty-four broad, both for the use of the governor; the latter was originally intended for a public promenade, and planted with fine trees, many of which yet remain."[10]

Many of these fine trees still shade the garden now known as the Governor's Garden, for many years past open to the public. Not a sunny summer day passes that groups of people do not stroll beneath those trees, leisurely admiring the incomparable view of river, island, cliffs, with the bright parade of promenaders on Dufferin Terrace immediately in the foreground of the panorama.

The Château Haldimand was destined to serve a very worth-

[10]1815.

while purpose later. It was to be not merely the "old Château" but the "only" château in Quebec—but that was not until 1834.

****

The wise administration of Sir John Coape Sherbrooke, who succeeded Prevost, was all too brief, covering the years 1816-1818. Characterized by great kindness of heart and solicitude for the unfortunate, he brought these human qualities to bear upon the unsettled status of Quebec politics; these, combined with his noble military bearing and quiet wisdom, would have had a soothing effect on the troubled waters of the political stream had he remained a little longer than two years. But colonial administration by England was still not what it should have been; Sherbrooke grew weary of it, began to suffer from ill health, and requested his recall.

****

The social world of Quebec had been rather quiet and uneventful since the Duke of Kent's departure twenty-four years previously. But now, once more, the city opened her arms to the splendour of a nobleman's presence. Charles Gordon Lennox, Duke of Richmond, Lennox and Aubigny, was a chivalrous gentleman whose political views had, however, been so carefully grooved along Tory lines in England that Canada was to be little, if any, better off, politically speaking, for his presence here.

Although far from being a young man, the Duke of Richmond gave the necessary impetus to the usual mad whirl of functions that the presence of a title seemed always to set in motion in Quebec. Once again the Château St. Louis echoed to the sounds of music and dancing. And something new had been added. The theatre, which had been so thoroughly squelched in the time of Frontenac, had been revived and the best of plays were now currently presented in the little theatre that formed an adjunct to the castle. There was, too, another exciting note: a racecourse had made its appearance on the plains of Abraham. . . !

The Duke arrived on July 29th, 1818, accompanied by his daughter, Lady Sarah, and her husband, Sir Peregrine Maitland, the latter having been appointed Lieutenant-Governor of Ontario.

A year later, on August 20th, 1819, while travelling through the woods in Ontario, near the little village of Richmond, which had been named after him, on a tour of inspection with a view to improving communications as well as defences, the Duke suddenly became violently ill. As the little party launched their canoes on the Rideau River, the Duke was seized by a frenzied paroxysm. The boatmen were scarcely able to land their boats again before the Duke wrenched himself from his attendants and ran wildly into the woods. An hour or so later they found him lying prostrate and almost unconscious on the damp ground, in the last throes of what was apparently hydrophobia. It then came to light that about two months previously the Governor had been bitten on the finger by a pet fox which had belonged to one of his attendants and which was not known to be rabid.

The Duke of Richmond died that very night in a rude camp hastily pitched by the roadside. And the little outing, begun so blithely, was converted into a funeral cortege to conduct the unfortunate nobleman back to Quebec and to his castle where he had been so merry and so much admired. For two days his body lay in state in the wide, high-ceilinged chamber of the Château St. Louis, while all Quebec—indeed, all Canada—mourned his passing. On September 4th, he was interred with great pomp and solemnity in the chancel of the English Cathedral of Quebec. A small brass plaque marks the spot:

Beneath
are deposited
the Mortal Remains of
Charles
Duke of Richmond,
Lennox and Aubigny,
the Monument to whose
Memory
is placed in the North Gallery
of this Church.

On the small marble monument are the words:

Sacred to the Memory of
Charles,
Fouth Duke of Richmond, Lennox and Aubigny,

Knight of the Most Honorable Order of the Garter;
Lord Lieutenant and Vice Admiral of the County of Sussex;
High Steward of the City of Chichester;
A General in the Army, and Colonel of the 35th Regiment,
and of the Royal Sussex Militia;
Governor General and Commander in Chief of Canada,
and over all His Majesty's possessions in North America,
Who died at Richmond, in Upper Canada,
on the 20th of August, 1819, in the 55th year of his age.

****

Chapter Eleven

IF THE HISTORY OF QUEBEC were a tapestry, how rich and variegated would be the colours, how incredibly intricate the design, how unusual the workmanship! Scarcely a year passed without some new twist of the thread, a deeper colour introduced; here and there the evidence of a careful hand; and here and there traces of a hand that gave all too little attention to ways of warp and weft, too little thought to the choice of colour and the quality of material. Thus Quebec would appear when examined in detail. But move back a pace or two—say, a hundred years or so—and the tapestry becomes a profound blend of all that makes the life of men and cities the splendid or sordid things they so often become. Turning the eyes to the tangled threads of today, one can assess the importance of all that has gone before and get the sharply subduing impression that because that was, this is.

In the year 1819, a bit of green was woven inextricably into the tapestry. Between twelve and thirteen thousand Irish, full of hope that the new land would be kinder to them than the old had been, came to Canada and settled in Quebec and its environs. Succeeding years found many more arriving, following friends and relatives already here — for here there was soil to call one's own . . . and food . . . and even if the shamrock would not flourish here, and even if the rivers were not as silvery as the Shannon, this was a good land. They have never found it otherwise. And because their faith was the faith of old Quebec, they mingled with the French-Canadians as the English had never done. Thus today we have Malones who speak more French than English and Héberts who speak English equally as well as French.

Before the arrival of the Irish in 1819, the population of Quebec was a little over fifteen thousand. In the city alone—including, of course, the fast-growing suburbs—there were two thousand houses.

From March to June of the year 1820, Sir Peregrine Maitland, recently Lieutenant-Governor of Ontario, acted as Administrator-in-Chief of the affairs of Canada; his wife, the charming Lady Sarah Lennox, daughter of the Duke of Richmond, was chatelaine of the Château St. Louis. Maitland was relieved of his charge by the arrival, in June, of the new Governor who was no less a personage than George, Ninth Earl of Dalhousie, an outstanding military man whose talents in the field of statesmanship were not less than on the field of battle.

To Lord Dalhousie, Canada owes the seed of an idea that has since borne important fruit. After looking deeply into matters disrupting the government and after doing his utmost to pacify the various insurgent factions, Lord Dalhousie suggested that much could be accomplished if Upper and Lower Canada would unite. It was without doubt an excellent suggestion but Canada was not yet ready for such a step. Eventually, however, when this had actually come to pass some fifteen years later, it was but natural that the union of all Canada should be considered. Because of Lord Dalhousie, the rising sun of Confederation glimmered on the horizon of Canada.

This Governor's activities were varied and numerous, and all greatly to his credit. Under his sponsorship and patronage, the Literary and Historical Society of Quebec was formed in the year 1824. It was instigated for the purpose of the "investigation of points of history immediately connected with the Canadas, to discover and rescue from the unsparing hand of time the records which yet remain of the earliest history of Canada, to preserve . . . such documents as may be found amid the dust of yet unexplored depositaries. . . ."

On Monday, March 15th, 1824, one of the first meetings of the Society was held in the Château St. Louis, and the by-laws were drawn up. The first officers were: His Excellency the Right Honourable George, Earl of Dalhousie, G.C.B., as Founder and patron; and as President, His Excellency the Honourable Sir Francis Burton, K.C.G., a former pro-tem administrator of Canada during a vacation taken by Lord Dalhousie in 1822. A Royal Charter, dated October 5th, 1831, formally incorporated the Society. Today this Society, the oldest of its kind in the British Empire Overseas, is one of Quebec's most cherished possessions; its library on St. Stanislas Street, in the building formerly Morin College, is a quiet and dearly-loved spot for the loyal members who support and guard its priceless contents.

As has been said in an earlier chapter, Lord Dalhousie sponsored the erection, by popular subscription, of the Wolfe-Montcalm monument in the garden beside the Château. The foundation for it was laid on November 15th, 1827. The ceremony of the laying of the foundation stone was a most colourful function which took place on a bright autumn day. At eleven o'clock in the morning, the garrison of the city formed a line along the street which separates the Governor's Garden from the Terrace. Members of the Grand Lodge of Masons turned out in full force in all the regalia of their Order. The band of the Sixty-Sixth Regiment filled the air with martial music. The Governor's lady and her entourage passed down the lane of military figures from the Château's gate to a vantage point near where the monument was to stand. Shortly afterwards, His Excellency took his place with appropriate ceremony, accompanied by his aides and personal staff as well as the Lord Bishop of Quebec and the Chief Justice.

The most touching part of the event was the appearance of a stately old gentleman who took a place of honour near Lord Dalhousie. This venerable patriarch of ninety-five years, leaning heavily on the arm of Captain Young, was Mr. James Thompson, the only living survivor in Quebec of the Battle of the Plains of Abraham. Sixty-eight years before he had been a loyal sergeant in the ranks of the victor, and since then had been a Building Supervisor (until his retirement) and had assisted in the building of the Château Haldimand in 1784-86. He it was who recorded the finding of the Malta Stone which was placed in the wall of that building and which now embellishes the Château Frontenac. In 1818, it was he who had been able to reveal reliably where General Montgomery had been buried in 1775 which enabled relatives to exhume the body for removal to New York.

Captain Young of the Seventy-Ninth Highlanders, on whose arm the old gentleman supported himself, was the designer of the splendid column of stone that was to be erected *in memoriam* to Wolfe and Montcalm. The climax of this ceremony was Mr.

Thompson's simple act of striking three times with a mallet on the foundation stone. This was probably the last appearance of this grand old gentleman for he was unable to appear at the unveiling of the monument less than a year later. He died in 1830 in his ninety-eighth year in the family mansion on old Ste. Ursule street which was subsequently occupied by his grandson, James Thompson Harrower.[1]

It so happened that the day of the unveiling was also the day of the departure of the Earl and Countess of Dalhousie from Canada: September 8th, 1828. It, too, was a most impressive and moving pageant, coupled as it was with the emotions of impending farewell. In the late afternoon of that cool September day, Sir James Kempt, the new Governor, escorted the retiring Governor and his lady from the Château St. Louis to the waiting ship, *H.M.S. Challenger*. Previously a lavish entertainment had been given them at which many expressions of esteem, and regret at the pending departure, had been voiced by the city's leading citizens. Lord Dalhousie was being recalled to take command in India.

Sir James Kempt was a quiet man, extremely sensitive. He may not actually have felt intimidated by the political agitators of the day but he devised a peculiar policy of dealing with them. Those who had caused Lord Dalhousie most trouble, Kempt zealously cultivated; those who had been nearest to his predecessor, Kempt carefully avoided. The result was that Quebec wondered exactly where the new Governor stood in the politics of Canada. His attitude misled no one for very long. His hypocritical methods were not lost upon the astute Frenchmen who soon perceived that his cordiality was but superficial.

Fortunately, before he had done much damage, Kempt was clever enough to realize his failure as an administrator of Canada's complex affairs, and requested his recall. His successor, Lord Matthew Whitworth Aylmer, arrived on October 13th, 1830, and Kempt departed very quietly, without pomp or fanfare, on the 30th of that month.

Lady Aylmer was a diarist; her account of their arrival in Quebec (in the form of a letter to a friend) is excellent. "You

[1]J. M. Le Moine in *Picturesque Quebec,* (1882).

may readily conceive our joyous feelings, when we sailed with a fair wind up the magnificent St. Lawrence, some idea of which scenery I hope some day to give you from drawings; the settlements on either side looking like an Encampment, the houses and roofs being white, backed by a mass of dark native woods of Fir and Maple, with other light trees mixed. Unfortunately, as we were going at the rate of ten or eleven knots an hour, we could not avoid anchoring at night under the Walls of Quebec, and miss'd seeing our future residence backed by the bold Cape Diamond; as we approached next morning very early, the young A.D.C.'s and the Governor appeared in full costume, and I daresay you would have thought with me when I decided they all looked very handsome, and I felt very proud of them. I certainly was not worthy of them for I could only get out a large black Beaver bonnet lined with pink, with black feathers, and a warm wadded silk cloak, as the weather, though bright and fine, seemed very cold. The salute on our quitting the *Herald,* and the yards manned with her beautiful ship's crew hurraing us as we left the ship, together with the many heartfelt expressions of good wishes and good will (for we had been so fortunate as to make many friends among the officers during our passage), all this went to my heart, and my nerves being weakened by illness, I had some difficulty in drying my eyes so as to meet Sir James Kempt with proper decorum; he came with his numerous staff to the landing, to receive, and led horses being brought for Lord Aylmer and staff. Sir James conducted me in his phaeton and four, up the steep hill to the Château St. Louis which is the Governor's residence. It was a beautiful sight I assure you, and we thought everything in and about the Château much more agreeable than we had expected, good sized rooms, good garden and green house, riding house, etc. . . . our suite of rooms look on the magnificent river St. Lawrence, at this moment frozen over, which is superstitiously supposed to occur when a new Governor arrives, and to be a good omen."

The people of Quebec greeted Lord Aylmer warmly, full of hope that he would follow in the steps of Lord Dalhousie. It was during Lord Aylmer's governorship, in the fourth year of his sojourn among Canadians, that Quebec suffered an irreparable loss. . . . But wait! Let us have a brief resumé of those four years. . . .

Lord Aylmer made an unfortunate beginning so far as Parliament was concerned. Rather thoughtlessly — tactlessly, it seems—he addressed the governing body as if they were no more than children, conveying the impression that he had come to show them how things should be done. This was faintly reminiscent of "Little King Craig", and there were those in Parliament who remembered *him* all to well. It took some little time for the political parties to recover from this condescending treatment, and by then it had added considerable impetus to the rebellion that was threatening under the leadership of the famous Louis Joseph Papineau—of whom we shall hear more anon.

Quebec had a gloriously gala day in the spring of 1831. On a fresh and bright April day, the first steamboat built in Canada was launched in the port of Quebec. A public holiday was proclaimed and the city was made festive with bunting and flags. People dressed in their Sunday best and gathered in crowds to listen to the bands and to watch and cheer as Lady Aylmer broke the customary bottle of champagne on the prow of the new vessel, christening it *Royal William*. Guns boomed in salute from the Citadel—and ushered in a new era of shipping on the great waters of the St. Lawrence.

Two years later, this same vessel left Quebec, on August 5th, 1833, and made the first crossing of the Atlantic by steam alone, taking nineteen and a half days.[2]

Among the records of the Parliamentary sessions of the time, we find that in 1831 the sum of £2,500 was voted for "repairing the ancient Castle of St. Lewis at Quebec". The Castle was in as constant need of repair as it had always been, even in the days of Comte de Frontenac. The Governors were constantly requesting money for repairs and renovations. To tear down the old castle; to take the money available to build something better in its place: such was unthinkable to the British—whose national tendency is to cherish a traditional ruin, even if its presence should be a reminder of a glorious history quite apart from the Empire; it had

[2]J. M. Le Moine in *The Port of Quebec, 1535-1900.*

become a symbol of England's colonial expansion and should be preserved at all costs. If it must be a ruin, then let it be a restored ruin. In this, the French of Canada heartily concurred since it concerned their beloved Château St. Louis. So, in the years 1831 to 1834, the Château underwent further operations at the cost of approximately three thousand pounds.

By 1832 the Imperial Government finished the fortifications of Quebec which had been commenced in 1823 on a plan of the Duke of Wellington. The walls built were those that stand today, which included as far as possible those built by the Comte de Frontenac, and which cause Quebec to be described today as "the only walled city in North America". The cost of the erection of the walls and the citadel was thirty-five million dollars.

"We were soon quite settled in our present habitation," writes Lady Aylmer, "and while Lord Aylmer was becoming acquainted with the duties of his new Government, I was occupied in trying to make our old Château look a little more like home, and finding better workmen than I had been led to expect in Quebec, I soon accomplished our wishes in this respect, and then began to try to perform my part, in our present understanding, by endeavouring to receive persons of all kinds, as if they were welcome, and we have as many dinners, parties, and balls, as could be introduced with any sort of regard to our own peace of mind and body."

In all ages, it seems, the eve of a New Year has been the cause of general celebration. It was no less so in Quebec. The newspaper, *Quebec Mercury,* of January 2nd, 1834, printed the following:

> "The close of the year 1833 and the commencement of 1834 were celebrated at the Castle of St. Louis by the Lady Aylmer being at home to a numerous party of civilians and military, who were entertained at a ball and supper in the old château. The guests began to arrive about nine o'clock and at ten dancing commenced with a country dance which was followed by quadrilles and waltzes till the supper room was thrown open at midnight, and the company repaired to tables laid out with the greatest taste and covered with every delicacy. After a moderate time spent at table, and the usual congratulations and compliments of the season, dancing was resumed and

kept up till a late hour of the morning; when the party broke up, after a scene of great festivity and pleasure, rather from a prudent recollection of the fatigue custom has associated with the first of January and to which all must submit, than from any feeling of lassitude or satiety of the pleasure they had enjoyed."[3]

****

As was customary during a session of Parliament, letters and documents, addresses and replies, went daily in and out of the Governor's chambers in the Castle, to and from the Parliament building. Matters of State were progressing more or less as usual during the January session of 1834—that is, until the bugles of the Castle gave the signal: Fire! The drums of the Citadel caught up the sound, and cries of "Fire! Fire!", shattered the noonday peace of Place d'Armes. Spirals of smoke were rising from the third story of the southern end of the ancient Château St. Louis. It was but a matter of minutes before the entire top floor of the building began to emit smoke, and the flames appeared on all sides. In spite of the equipment of the city's fire department, the fire brigade, the troops and citizenry, the fire spread downward with disheartening rapidity and began to consume the whole building.

The fire had broken out in one of the apartments of the Governor's aides: that of Captain McKinnon, who, fortunately, escaped any injury. Lord and Lady Aylmer, their personal staff and guards, were able to leave the building in plenty of time. The official documents, the Governor's valuable silver, china, paintings, furniture and other treasured belongings, were nearly all safely removed with as little damage as possible. Had it been summer-time, the fire might have been checked before the wonderful old place was absolutely gutted—but it was winter, very much winter! and the engines and hoses were shortly frozen and useless in the sub-zero weather.

What a sight it must have been to see that great pile of stone and timber, set high upon a hill, all ablaze against the early twilight sky of a Quebec winter! But a heartbreaking sight, too, when one recalled all that the castle had stood for through so

[3] *The Quebec Mercury*, January 2nd, 1834.

many long years, all the toiling and scheming, the care and patience, the money it had cost, the historic events it had witnessed; two hundred years vanishing in smoke. Were the ghosts of Champlain, Montmagny, Frontenac, and the others, hovering near the ruins of the Château St. Louis on that bleak and bitter night of January 23rd, when their handiwork lay obliterated by the cruel fingers of fire? Some say that Frenchmen wept in Quebec that night. . . .

As one of Quebec's newspapers afterwards remarked in its write-up of the conflagration: "much of that disaster is to be regretted; it is nevertheless consolatory to reflect the season of the year, and the protection that the snow afforded to the roofs of the closely built houses in the Lower Town immediately below it, averted the incalculable mischief which might otherwise have been occasioned in that quarter.

"The thermometer on the morning of the fire had marked twenty-two degrees below zero, and during the whole time it (the fire) lasted, it continued from two degrees to eight degrees below zero, with a strong piercing wind from west to south west. Many of the engines were soon frozen up, and the hose and everything connected with them, could only be kept in anything like order by the use of warm water which was generously furnished from the breweries of Messrs. Racey, McCallum, and Quirouet, and by the religious communities. The citizens and troops distinguished themselves by their services; but from the impossibility of reaching the part of the building overlooking the precipice, it soon became apparent that any successful attempt to arrest the progress of the flames was hopeless. It will probably cost £25,000 to £30,000 to erect a new building, but the beauty of the situation, and the extent of the grounds, will afford an opportunity of erecting one of the most ornamental and prominent public buildings in the city of which Quebec is really lamentably deficient. The site belongs to the Military Government."

The chilling night winds whined through the charred and ruined masonry; snow whirled in small white drifts around the blackened chimneys and fireplaces, hastened to hide the bereft buttresses, the heaps of rubble, which were all that was left of the Château St. Louis, as though Winter itself lamented the loss and were trying to cool and cover the wounds that fire had made.

Meanwhile, the Governor, temporarily located in the residence of the Honourable Colonel Gore, Deputy Quarter-Master-General to the Forces, penned the following historic words to the Parliamentary Assembly:

> "The Governor-in-Chief regrets to have to inform you that the ancient castle of St. Lewis, occupied by him as an official residence, caught fire yesterday, soon after noon, and that notwithstanding the efforts of his Majesty's troops, the Worshipful Mayor of Quebec, the gentlemen of the seminary, the fire companies, and a large concourse of citizens of every class, who repaired with alacrity to the spot, and were unceasing in their exertions to save that public building from destruction, it was entirely consumed.
>
> 24th January, 1834."

****

Chapter Twelve

WHAT WAS IT LIKE in Quebec without the old Château St. Louis? Where did the Governor and his Lady reside? Where were their social functions held? What was done about those blackened walls that stood as a bleak souvenir of past glories.

Fortunately, thanks to the good Sir Frederick Haldimand, Quebec had a château to fall back on in time of need: the Château Haldimand—*le vieux château.* It has been noted that Sir Frederick built it in 1784 as an adjunct to the Château St. Louis which had proven inadequate to meet the needs of the Governor of a fast-growing Canada. It had been used principally for offices, meetings and public functions. In the period between 1808 and 1811, Governor Sir James Henry Craig had extensively enlarged the Château St. Louis, and thereafter the Château Haldimand was not used to such a great extent, and was, from that time onwards, called "the Old Château". But then the fire of 1834 left it the only château in Quebec and once more it sprang to life, this time to replace the Château St. Louis; it began to be referred to as the "Castle of St. *Lewis*" in the political documents, letters and newspapers of the period.

The rudely-evicted Governor and his Lady had moved (as has been noted) to the house of Colonel Gore where Lord Aylmer was confined for nearly three weeks with a severe cold caught on the day of the fire. When he had recovered, he and Lady Aylmer and their immediate suite took up residence "in the house of Mr. A. Hale, adjoining that of the Hon. John Hale" which was "the second from the last in the range facing the Governor's Garden and the harbour."[1] At that time, a building of public offices, located at the lower end of Place d'Armes was taken over in part by the Governor, his advisors and secretaries, for the conducting of official business.

The Château Haldimand, between the years 1834 and 1892, occupied alone the summit of the rock of Quebec. The Aylmers

[1]*The Quebec Mercury,* 1834.

never lived there, for it had not been built as a residence and considerable work and expense would have had to be expended on it to make it so. As far as can be ascertained, they remained in Mr. Hale's house until their departure from Canada on September 17th, 1835.

Life seems to have gone quite smoothly after the excitement of the fire in January, 1834. As soon as the Aylmers were comfortably accommodated and recovered from the shock and inconvenience they had suffered, they gave their usual levées, balls, suppers and 'at homes', that made them so popular and Quebec so bright and happy a place to live—providing, of course, that one had the *entrée* to the Castle and had been presented at the vice-regal Court.

The Press of the period gives a lively account of the doings at one such function held at the Château Haldimand almost a year after the fire, on December 31, 1834,[2] "Wednesday evening being the last day of the old year, Lady Aylmer was 'at home' in the Old Castle to those ladies and gentlemen who had the entrée. The company began to assemble shortly after nine o'clock, and before ten the ballroom was filled. Dancing began with a country dance, which her Ladyship led down, and Quadrilles and Waltzes followed to the music of the excellent orchestra formed by the band of the 79th Highlanders. A handsome supper was laid out in the dining-room and although the arrangements and alterations which have been made, have curtailed the dimensions of this apartment, the tables were so well arranged and so frequently recovered, that the lost space was only felt as the guests supped in successive parties and the ballroom was thinned for a longer time. Dancing was kept up with great spirit and it is many years since a new year had, at its birth, witnessed an assemblage of happy guests within the Old Castle of St. Lewis."

Then there was the lovely ball given by Lady Aylmer in honour of the birthday of Her Majesty the Queen, on February 24th, 1835, which was one of the social highlights of the year. Another was given in honour of His Majesty the King, in April,

[2]*The Quebec Mercury*, January 3rd, 1835.

which was also enormously successful. The ballroom was tastefully decorated with the colours of the four regiments of Canadian Militia; the Standard of the Quebec Troops of Light Dragoons formed a background for the orchestra; above the doors were the colours of the 32nd and 79th Regiments.

In June of that year, Aylmer was recalled. He had been suffering from ill health, and the political problems of the time had borne heavily upon him; his administration had not been an easy one; his judgments had not always satisfied the Home Government and certainly not the Assembly of Lower Canada. His conduct, however, had been flawless and exemplary even under the most trying conditions, and it is believed he was most conscientious in those instances where one political faction or another accused him of being otherwise. An editorial in a Quebec paper, commenting on Lord Aylmer's recall, remarks of his administration that there "was little to condemn and much to approve".[3]

Lady Aylmer had found her own special niche in the hearts of the people of Quebec. She had entertained them; she had been entertained by them; she had visited their schools, their hospitals, their poor. Her diary is full of gentle observations on Canada and Canadians. She was deeply appreciative of the beauties of Quebec. "This morning my usual spring wakefulling, together with the heat, aroused me at four o'clock and finding that I could not sleep I sat by the window watching the glorious rising of the sun over the opposite hills, and throwing his broad light in bright red over the magnificent river covered with ships just come, and coming in, from Great Britain, bringing us settlers and merchandise; this scene is indeed lovely and deserves to be studied. . . ." Lady Aylmer had seen what few *Quebecois* (or their guests) ever see: a scene of unearthly glory, defying description or reproduction: dawn and sunrise on the St. Lawrence, bathing old Quebec in fantastic radiance. . . .

Naturally, before the popular couple left Canada, social functions were more than ever the order of the day. The Attorney-General, Mr. Ogden, and Mrs. Ogden, put on a *fête champêtre* on

[3]*The Quebec Gazette,* June 26th, 1835.

August 6th, a most magnificent occasion that rivalled anything the Aylmers had done in their most elaborate efforts.

But the "Parting Ball and Supper" outdid and outshone everything yet done in Quebec under the British régime! Adjoining the Old Château, a theatre had been devised out of a former riding school and drill hall, and currently the greatest artists and actors on the continent, as well as groups of local talent, displayed their thespian abilities there. It was known as the Theatre Royale St. Louis. On the occasion of the "Parting Ball", it was used to entertain six hundred people to do farewell honours to the departing Governor and his Lady. The entrance walk was a covered way from street to door for the event, and was lined by a Guard of Honour of the 66th and 79th Regiments. The rooms were lavishly decorated and brilliantly lighted. The elegantly attired throng—the dress costumes of the period were so dashing and colourful!—that moved gracefully to and fro beneath the gently swaying bunting and flags must have afforded a feast for the eyes had it been possible for anyone to creep unseen into the balcony above. A roll of drums . . . the floor cleared to allow the Guests of Honour to proceed to lead the first contradance; the assembly followed; then there were waltzes, gallopades, quadrilles. . . . It was as if old Vienna had come to Quebec. Supper was a magical and dazzling display; the side scenes and drapes of the stage were parted to reveal, as if at a wave of an enchanted hand, tables laden with crystal, fine china, pure white linen, sparkling silver, and every possible edible delicacy. And then, as if this feasting was not enough, the company rose once more and danced far into the night.

Was the spirit of Frontenac hovering in the wings, then, too, reminiscing on the gatherings he had held in the same city so long ago? And was the spirit of the harassed and lonely Champlain somewhere there, sadly comparing the festive board with that of the roots and dried peas that he had shared with his people?

The next day the newspapers' comments went something like this: "There was not heard, during the whole time, a word that might have had a distant allusion to the public difficulties of the country. It was a free and undisguised interchange of the polished and agreeable intercourse of life."[4]

The Earl of Gosford, Baron Worlingham of Beccles, was appointed Captain-General and Governor-in-Chief of the Provinces of Upper and Lower Canada, etc., to succeed Lord Aylmer. He was duly sworn in by Lord Aylmer on August 24th, at a Council held in the ballroom of the Castle.

And then the Aylmers sailed away. The pomp of their departure was brilliant beyond description — but, after all, no more than expected after the preceding celebrations. The Governor left his residence on horseback, accompanied by a mounted military guard; Lady Aylmer left in her private carriage accompanied by the wives of the dignitaries of government.

"The day was beautifully serene, with scarce a breath of wind." The procession moved with becoming stateliness; past the old Château and the ruins of the Château that had once been their home; through Prescott Gate; down Mountain Hill; along the street of Notre Dame, to the King's Wharf where the Grenadiers of the 79th Highlanders formed a Guard of Honour.

The whole city turned out *en masse* to say goodbye. People lined the heights and the streets and the wharves and the shore, Guns boomed in salute from the Citadel and the band of the 66th Regiment struck up the nostalgic air, "Auld Lang Syne". By mid-afternoon, Their Excellencies were safely aboard *H.M.S. Pique,* and as the breeze came up stronger, the sails broke and filled, and the splendid vessel moved slowly away towards the horizon.

****

Lord Gosford was a different type of man to Lord Aylmer. He was not possessed of the same warm spontaneity, the zest for living that had characterized Lord Aylmer. Perhaps he took his political duties more seriously than Lord Aylmer but history does not record that he was any more successful in them than his predecessor had been.

After settling in the Old Château (which he had chosen to be his residence and which had been duly fitted for the purpose), Lord Gosford proceeded to give the populace of Canada the surprise of

[4]*The Quebec Gazette,* September 16th, 1835.

its life. He had the temerity to have as his guests for dinner and a chat a certain Mr. Louis Joseph Papineau and his cohorts. The people were further confounded by the absence of any information, official or otherwise, as to what had been discussed over the diner table.

This event was followed a few weeks later by a ball and supper at the Château in honour of the fête of Ste. Catherine. This was (and is today) a popular fête among the French-Canadians on which they make and eat a sweet confection called *la tir,* consisting of molasses boiled to a certain point, allowed to cool slightly, taken in the hands and drawn and pulled until it is a creamy white colour and delicious to eat; in present-day parlance: a taffy-pull. (One wonders if milord and his guests did "pull taffy" of one kind or another that evening).

A meaningful word or two in the newspapers is considerably enlightening as to the dubious success of this affair: ". . . many persons who have had the entrée to those particular parties, upon which the etiquette of our fashionable world has usually been formed, were a good deal surprised to find themselves strangers to nearly half the company. His Excellency's obliging manner has, we are afraid, undertaken a hard task, to make such assemblages enjoy themselves freely and associate together; for of all things most difficult to overcome, are the vanities and distinctions of life, which, whether ill- or well-founded, exist everywhere, and what may be thought odd by some, in no place more so than in North America."[5]

In December, 1835, Lord Gosford opened the Legislature with all the traditional ceremony—and made a speech that was "ill received by all parties".

The usual New Year's Eve ball and supper were given by His Excellency at the close of 1835. It was a happy celebration, well attended and lasting into the early hours of 1836. The best of food and wines were served in abundance, and toasts were drunk frequently and deeply—too deeply, if one assesses the implication of a series of small advertisements which appeared in subsequent issues of the *Quebec Mercury*:

[5]*The Quebec Gazette,* November 23rd, 27th, 1835.

LOST

Taken from the Castle of St. Lewis yesterday morning, a Blue Cloth Cloak, lined with black serge, having a small cape similarly lined, a black Velvet Collar with rounded ends and gilt clasps in the shape of lion's feet, and a small triangular "Fly" on the upper part of the right side of the cloak.

LOST

Blue Cloak, plain, and a small Seal Skin Cap.

LOST

An Otter Skin Cap.

And then there appeared a notice calling a meeting at the local Court House of all who had lost articles at the "Castle of St. Lewis" on the first morning of the New Year.

The year 1836 heard the first rumblings of the forthcoming uprising of French Canada against rule by Great Britain. The elections which took place that year were characterized by mob action —in fact, during the spring, Montreal was for brief periods practically in the possession of mobs when "no English or Irish workman dared to return to his home alone".[6]

By 1837, the rebellion really got underway, and Mr. L. J. Papineau became a hero to most of the populace of Lower Canada and an enemy to the rest. The period of brooding over the old defeat, and its termination of French dominion in Canada, was over. Now was the time for active and forceful expression of these long-repressed feelings.

The rebellion had its inception as far back as 1805 over taxation. When this was settled, language became a contending issue. By 1813 Papineau rose as a leader of the French *Patriotes* and awoke the French-Canadians to awareness that, compared to members of the British House of Commons, they had neither power nor position, that the British Executive Council voted all monies for civil expenditure in Canada which might well be done by the Canadian House of Assembly. He was further aroused when, in 1822, the British Union Bill attempted to unite the two Canadas.

[6]*The Quebec Gazette,* March 5th, 1836.

Against Lord Dalhousie, then Governor of Canada, Papineau voiced his displeasure in Parliament. The Governor refused to recognize Papineau's appointment as Speaker of the House, demanded that the Assembly reconsider their choice. When the Assembly refused, Dalhousie dissolved the House.

In 1834, the *Patriotes* drew up their platform, their Declaration of Rights, the Ninety-Two Resolutions, a rebellious bid for redress of wrongs, including a demand for the recall of Lord Aylmer who had recently been made Governor.

But Papineau, now blinded by his own achievements, met every overture of peace with suspicion. Though Canada needed Responsible Government, he saw it as a deprivation of the rights of the French-Canadian. In the years 1837-38, riots broke out wherever meetings were held. The Press whetted the zeal of both factions. Papineau's violence waxed more unreasonable; by his own ill-considered actions, he lost the confidence of many of his followers, among them two influential citizens of Quebec City, Elzear Bédard, who had moved the Ninety-Two Resolutions, and Etienne Parent, editor of *Le Canadien.* Their secession brought a revulsion of feeling in Quebec, and thus the City escaped the hostilities of the late months of 1837.

A warrant was issued, by Lord Gosford, for Papineau's arrest on a charge of high treason, and he fled to the United States. A price of four thousand dollars was offered for information as to his whereabouts. Defiantly, one of the rebels, Doctor Masson, offered a reward of one hundred pounds for Lord Gosford's head!

Papineau remained in the United States while the revolts he had instigated took the lives of many of his followers. The rebellion reached its climax between November 17th and December 14th, 1837. Of the thousands who had taken part in the revolt, scarcely a hundred were brought to trial; of the twelve executed, none were the ring-leaders; they fled the country. Papineau returned to Canada in 1845. In 1847 he was again in Parliament.

Lord Gosford, at his own suggestion, was recalled early in 1838. He felt Canada could no longer be served by his conciliatory measures. Between his departure and the arrival of Lord Durham, Sir John Colborne administered Canada's affairs.

Chapter Thirteen

HER MAJESTY'S SHIP *Hastings* cast anchor below Quebec on Mary 27th, 1838, after a run of thirty-two days out of Portsmouth. On board were His Excellency the Governor-in-Chief the Right Honourable the Earl of Durham, the Countess of Durham, their family and suite. They landed the following day and were warmly welcomed by a cheering populace, the salute of guns from the Citadel and flags waving at every corner and window.

The regal procession moved up Mountain Hill, past the Château Haldimand, and on to the Globe Hotel (once situated at No. 11 St. Louis street, on land now covered by the Château Frontenac) where the finest apartments the house possessed had been put in readiness for their use. The Earl and Countess of Durham remained there thirteen days while other quarters were being prepared for them in a wing of the Parliament Buildings. We can well imagine how proud and honoured was the proprietor of that hotel, Mr. Adam Schluep, to have such noble guests in his establishment.

While in Canada the Durhams lived in an edifice that was one of the oldest in Quebec but which today does not exist. Situated on the small space of ground now known as Montmorency-Laval Park, which possesses one of the most excellent views in the city from the top of Mountain Hill, this building had successively been a Bishop's Palace, and a House of Assembly forming part of the Legislative Buildings of Lower Canada. Prior to Lord Durham's arrival, it was elaborately conditioned and fitted for living quarters worthy of the King's representative. In a disastrous fire in February, 1854, these buildings were destroyed.

Symbolic of the changes that were to follow in Lord Durham's wake was his first political act of dismissing the Executive Council for an indefinite time since he deemed its abolition to be essential to the object of his mission. That mission was to look deeply into Canadian affairs and to report at length on them to the British

Government. In his dual office of Governor-in-Chief and Royal High Commissioner, Lord Durham had unlimited powers to suppress discord. It was fortunate that he already had had extensive experience in public office for it was to serve him well in Canada.

And now, once again, Quebec set out upon a round of social activities. This time it was, more than ever before, the equivalent of the Court of St. James. Every ceremony, every etiquette, every protocol, was strictly observed according to the manner of the Home Court. The first levée held by the Durhams, though conducted similarly to all such functions, was a studied example of stateliness and ritual. The people of Quebec were much impressed —which, after all, was probably what was intended by such displays of Court effulgence.

In his book *The Port of Quebec, 1535-1900,* J. M. Le Moine writes, "There never was so grand a display of vice-regal pomp, naval and military pageantry at Quebec; never were the Château *levées,* receptions and balls more decorously attended, (the Windsor ceremonies having this year been introduced); never in fact, was our spacious port studded in such profusion with the panoply of naval warfare since the flag of Britain floats on our waters, as during the summer of 1838. On the 29th of May there had landed at the Queen's Wharf, amidst excited crowds, one of England's proudest noblemen, the Earl of Durham, from *H.M.S. Hastings,* escorted by a stately line of battleships, frigates, gunboats, etc. The Earl was deputed by the Queen as Governor-General and High Commissioner to administer Canada and report on its state."

The brief visit of Lord and Lady Durham was the brightest period the city had known since the departure of the Aylmers.

A great deal has been written on Durham's work in Canada; some writers eulogize what he tried to do; others criticize what he did do; but all admit that the task that confronted him was such that he could not reasonably have satisfied everyone, both in Canada and in England, regardless of the course he pursued. For five months he strove to achieve the purpose for which he had been sent here. Then, abruptly, he was recalled, and left Canada on November 1st, 1838.[1]

[1]Date given by *Canadian Historical Review,* Vol. XX, 1939.

An eye-witness account of the departure of Lord and Lady Durham from Quebec has been left us by Mr. Charles Buller, Secretary to Lord Durham, in *Sketch of Lord Durham's Mission to Canada in 1838.*[2] "A sad day and a sad departure it was. The streets were crowded; the spectators filled every window and every house-top; and, though every hat was raised as we passed, a deep silence marked the general grief for Lord Durham's departure. . . . He did not expect to reach England alive . . . sickened by the malignity and weakness of which he had been the victim. . . . As the frigate bore Lord Durham out of the harbour the sky was black with clouds bearing the first snowstorm of the winter, and hardly a breath of air was moving. . . ."

****

The cause of the sudden and unexpected recall of the Governor was Lord Melbourne's[3] refusal to sanction Lord Durham's act of banishing eight Canadian rebels to Bermuda instead of allowing them to be brought to trial—which would without doubt have ended in a hanging, thereby adding fuel to the fires of racial hatred in Canada.

Lord Durham's report to his Government was a detailed and noteworthy account of Canada's affairs, political and otherwise, and perhaps it was not his fault—but rather his misfortune—that it was not all his government had hoped it would be. After all, five months was scarcely sufficient time to discern and report on all that impaired Canada at that time, much less to have studied it enough to take steps to remedy the conditions. The very fact that Durham was recalled before his mission was complete was, in itself, evidence of the Home Government's vacillation and indecision in colonial matters.

Two years after he reached home, Lord Durham was dead. And his last words on Canada were: "Canada will someday do justice to my memory."[4] Today there are few names in Canadian history more honoured than that of Lord Durham.

****

[2]This "Sketch" is found in *Lord Durham's Report* by Sir C. P. Lucas, (1912) Vol. 3, p. 370.

[3]Then Prime Minister of Great Britain.

[4]*The Canadian Historical Review,* Vol. XX, 1939.

In this story of the castles of Quebec and the beauties that pertained to them, the name of Lord Durham finds a special corner. To him Quebec is forever indebted for the splendid idea of a terrace, a promenade, along the brow of the heights overlooking the city. Though today this terrace no longer bears his name but that of one of his successors, Lord Dufferin, who lengthened and elaborated it, it still remains a symbol of Durham's thoughtfulness. In order to accomplish this terrace, Durham caused to be removed the unsightly portions of the ruins of the Château St. Louis; the buttresses, which had supported that building on the river side, were repaired to support the terrace; and the whole was covered by a platform which, together with the old-fashioned Governor's Garden adjoining the Old Château, was thrown open to the public.

Less than a quarter of the length of the present terrace, reaching only to within a few feet of the second kiosk, (there are now five kiosks: Victoria, Louise, Lorne, Frontenac and Plessis), Durham's Terrace was probably some two hundred feet long and about sixty feet in breadth. The Governor-General who had it lengthened to its present size—about 1,450 feet—was the Earl of Dufferin, whose name it now bears. At two o'clock on the afternoon of October 18th, 1878, forty years after Durham's first promenade was built, the Earl of Dufferin officiated at the laying of the cornerstone of the new terrace. In the stone he placed a leaden box containing portraits of himself and Lady Dufferin, as well as other mementoes of the occasion; he then gave the stone the customary *coup de grace* with a silver mallet. Some of the distinguished guests who witnessed this fine civic function were Dean Stanley of London; Count El Conde de Premio Real, Consul General of Spain; R. R. Dobell, Esq., of the Canadian Pacific Railway Company; and J. M. Le Moine, Canadian author and historian.

On July 9th, 1879, after the extensive alterations had been completed, Dufferin Terrace was opened to the public by His Excellency the Marquis of Lorne and Her Royal Highness the Princess Louise. The Marquis of Lorne had succeeded the Earl of Dufferin as Governor-General.

Today, this Terrace, or boardwalk, one hundred and eighty-two feet above the level of the St. Lawrence River that sweeps below it, is one of the scenic attractions of the city of Quebec, and of a summer night a band concert, a clear moon, gay couples on the soft green lawns, create a restful and charming diversion for all who care to share in its simple contentment.

****

It is October, 1840, and once more the frigate *H.M.S. Pique* crosses the Atlantic to bring a Governor-General to Canada. This time it is a personage little known in Canada but destined, nevertheless, to be widely known ere his tragic end puts a full stop to his useful activities. He is the Right Honourable C. Poulett Thompson, shortly to be created Baron of Sydenham, Kent and Toronto. He, too, spends his first night in Quebec in a hotel—Mr. Adam Schluep's Globe Hotel.

Mr. Thompson was a striking man of about forty years of age, and his appearance alone caused a flattering twitter wherever he went. He had received excellent training for his new position, having been head of the British Board of Trade, which had endowed him with confidence and a knowledge of the inner workings of the British cabinet. And before him lay the monumental task of building up Canada's government along the lines of that of Britain. Let it now be said that he acquitted himself of this task with success and honour.

In an address made by the magistrates of the city of Quebec to Mr. Thompson upon his arrival, an appeal was made to him for his support in their earnest ambition to have Quebec chosen as the capital of Canada. The diplomatic new Governor-General replied "that it would afford him the sincerest satisfaction . . . to reside within its walls whenever circumstances permitted."

One cannot help but smile at the eagerness of the people of Quebec to have the Governor-General reside among them when they had not, as yet, any proper and suitable abode to offer him, and when he had occasion to be in Quebec he would have only the Château Haldimand at his disposal which, as we have said before, was far from convenient for a residence.

The current topic of interest in these years was the problem of where—oh where?—the seat of government was to be. Quebec? Montreal? Toronto? Kingston? Bytown (Ottawa)? . . . By the process of elimination, Ottawa was first to drop from the list; next fell Toronto and Quebec; and the choice lay between Montreal and Kingston. In 1841, Queen Victoria chose Kingston and the argument seemed settled—at least, for the time being. But Quebec refused to accept elimination for she felt herself possessed of all the qualifications and requisites necessary for a Canadian capital—all, that is, except a house for the Governor-General.

In a last attempt to rectify this great drawback, the citizens of the old city, in 1842, held meeting after meeting of their Municipal Corporation to decide what, if anything, could be done about rebuilding the Château St. Louis. Eventually the City Council drew up the following resolution:

> "That it would be creditable to this city, and honourable alike both to the Provincial and Metropolitan Governments, that the Castle of St. Lewis should be rebuilt and rendered in all respects a suitable residence for the Governor-General during his sojourn in the ancient Capital of the British North American Provinces,
>
> "That owing to the unfortunate misunderstanding which then (referring to the eighteen thirties) existed between the Legislature and Executive Councils, and the fortuitous circumstances which have subsequently agitated the Province, its restoration (Castle of St. Lewis) has been delayed,
>
> "That inasmuch as harmony is now restored, and conceiving as the Council does, that it is the duty, and that it would be for the honour and dignity of the Provincial Government, that the Castle of St. Lewis should be rebuilt for the purposes originally intended,
>
> "Resolved,
>
> "That a Memorial to this effect be prepared and transmitted to His Excellency the Governor-General, Sir Charles Bagot, praying that it may be laid before the Legislature at its next session. . . ."[5]

There is no evidence that this Memorial was ever sent to Sir Charles Bagot (Lord Sydenham's successor). A minute perusal of the Journals of the Legislative Assembly of 1842 reveal that no such matter was at that time dealt with by the Assembly in Session.

[5] *The Quebec Mercury*, February 24th and March 19th, 1842.

Mr. Ernest Gagnon, in his book *Le Fort et Château St. Louis*, tells us that "plans were drawn up to this effect (reconstruction of the Château) but the project never materialized".

Lord Sydenham had all but worked himself out of existence. He was far from well and suffered intensely from gout which, upon one occasion at least, was so serious as to compel him to postpone the opening of the Legislature until he had recovered. In spite of this affliction he worked constantly, never giving his constitution a chance to recover. And so, when he was thrown from his horse and suffered a broken leg, his health collapsed completely. The gout which possessed his limbs inflamed the injury and a few days later the tragic symptoms of lockjaw appeared.

On a quiet Sunday morning in September, 1841, Lord Sydenham died. His last words to Canada, written as he endured every pain with most admirable fortitude, were much less bitter than those of Lord Durham! "May Almighty God prosper your labours and pour down upon this province all those blessings which in my heart I am desirous that it should enjoy."[6]

Canada owes much to Lord Sydenham. In the twenty-three months he was Governor-General, he set in motion that which all Canada had been striving to attain: Responsible Government.

❋❋❋❋❋❋❋❋❋❋❋❋

Sir Charles Bagot was Governor-General from 1841 to 1843. Although not a strong man physically, Sir Charles was firm willed and possessed excellent judgment, and to him belongs the credit for first establishing in practice the principles of responsible government. He died in the Spring of 1843, at Alwington House, Kingston, Ontario. He was succeeded by Sir Charles Metcalfe who made himself outstanding as the last of the Governors-General to attempt a personal government in Canada. Contrary to the rules of the new system, Metcalfe considered it his prerogative to make appointments to government offices without consulting his Council.

Lord Metcalfe was relieved of his position and succeeded by Charles Murray, Earl of Cathcart, as administrator. The Earl was made Governor-General on January 29th, 1847. In spite of this governor's efforts to follow the procedures outlined by Sir Charles

[6]Adam Shortt in *Lord Sydenham* (Makers of Canada Series).

Bagot, it was left to his successor, the Earl of Elgin and Kincardine, to give the new system the impetus it seemed to require.

A former Lieutenant-Governor of New Brunswick, Sir Edmund Walker Head, succeeded the Baron Elgin. His term was disturbed by the feuding antagonism of Upper and Lower Canada.

Sir Charles Stanley, fourth Viscount Monck, was made Governor-General of British North America in 1861, succeeding Lord Elgin. He played an active and energetic part in bringing about Confederation of the Provinces of Canada in 1867. He was succeeded by Lord Lisgar (Sir John Young) on December 29th, 1869. Lord Lisgar had recently (1861-1867) been Governor-General of New South Wales, Australia, and had there earned for himself a reputation of ability and wisdom which were brilliantly exercised to Canada's advantage.

The Earl of Dufferin succeeded Lord Lisgar in 1872. "It was confidently predicted that the people of Canada would appreciate the unaffected simplicity and sincerity of Lord Dufferin's declaration that to serve his country had always been the great passion of his life."[7] The record of his Canadian years leaves no doubt that the Earl served his country well.

****

In spite of the efforts of the citizens of Quebec, their city was never again to be the capital of the Dominion of Canada. The Governors-General who came to Canada in the succeeding years usually landed in Quebec or perhaps visited there on the occasion of some special civic function, but otherwise the gubernatorial chapter for Eastern Canada was closed.

Deprived of the pomp and ceremony of the Parliamentary Assemblages and functions, Quebec began to look to herself for entertainment and social life. The English sport of cricket made its appearance in the little French city, and matches in which English and French joined were held on the Plains of Abraham where once their forefathers had fought to the death for its possession.

In 1841 the first band concert was held on Durham Terrace. (The name of the Terrace had not then been altered.) Races

[7]William Leggo in *The History of the Administration of the Right Honorable Frederick Temple, Earl of Dufferin, in Canada.*

were held annually on the Plains of Abraham, and occasionally there was a running of the Queen's Plate. Regattas made the sparkling St. Lawrence a gay and gaudy river that would have amazed Champlain and delighted Frontenac.

Then there was the theatre. For some years the Coldstream Guards, garrisoned in Quebec, had been given permission to use the upper floors of the drill hall, adjoining the *Old Château* (Haldimand), as a theatre. The same quarters had witnessed the farewell ball and supper given for Lord and Lady Aylmer in 1835. Under the auspices of the Guards, excellent performances were given regularly, and when a new actor or actress made an appearance there, all Quebec patronized the Theatre Royale St. Louis. That is, until June 12th, 1846.

On this particular evening, Mr. Harrison from Hamilton, Ontario, a well known actor of the period, was giving of his best for the entertainment of Quebec. By ten o'clock his performance was over and the satisfied audience rose to go home. Suddenly a camphene lamp, suspended from the ceiling, broke away from the rafters to which it was affixed and crashed onto the stage. In a matter of seconds the curtains were ablaze, and the audience, with panic-stricken screams, flung itself as a single body towards the only exit. It was a narrow passageway down a short flight of steps—and the door opened inwardly! The mass of people, in frenzied haste to get away from the flames, pitched solidly against the door and penned themselves in. No one could force the door inward and there was no retreat. More than fifty persons, men, women and children, died that summer night in the Theatre Royale St. Louis

Mr. P. G. Roy tells us[8] that the Abbé Bernard O'Reilly, who later became Monsignor O'Reilly but was at that time Vicar of the Cathedral, was among the audience on that evening and that when he was observed by the doomed crowd, they cried to him for absolution; that a few moments or so after he had raised his hand in blessing, the Abbé was enabled to free himself.

The tragedy is often given as the reason for so many—in fact, most—doors in Quebec opening outwardly. In a city of streets scarcely wide enough for convenience, a pedestrian is in constant

[8]P. G. Roy, *Le Vieux Quebec.*

danger of being struck by a door as he passes by. But then, one has only to remember that fire of June 12th, 1846, when fifty lives might have been saved if a single door had opened outward!

****

The Old Château suffered a badly damaged wall in the fire but seemed otherwise unaffected by the tragic occurrence. The Municipality, obviously lacking a City Hall, occupied the Château for offices at that time and until 1851. The Department of Crown Lands occupied the ground floor; the Department of Public Works was on the upper floor; and the Provincial Registrar was in the old vaulted rooms of the Ammunition Store—the erstwhile powder magazine, to which we have earlier alluded as having been built by the Marquis de Denonville, Governor of New France in the years 1685-1689, as a part of the original Fort St. Louis.

In the period 1851-1854, the Château Haldimand was considerably repaired. In an appendix to his book *Quebec Past and Present* (1876), Sir James Le Moine says that the cost of repairs on this occasion was "£7,980,174". Undoubtedly the last three figures are in error for it is certain that a sum of this size could not be absorbed in repairs to such a building. In 1857 still more repairs were made when the Laval Normal School and Model Schools were established there. The vaulted rooms of the powder magazine—with little respect to their antiquity—were used as a kitchen for the school. Sir James tells us that "the Old Château was, by Order in Council of 14th February, 1871, transferred by the Dominion authorities to the Government of the Province of Quebec, together with Durham Terrace. . . ."

An event of international interest took place in July, 1855, when there was unveiled, on the outskirts of Quebec City, the St. Foye monument to the heroes of the Battle of Ste. Foye fought in April, 1760, as an aftermath to the Battle of the Plains of Abraham, where French troops, once defeated on the Plains, rallied and fought again for their country only to go down once more in defeat with loss of life on both sides. The monument is dedicated *To the Brave*, and is crowned by a statue of Bellona which was a gift of Prince Napoleon Bonaparte III. Upon the occasion of its unveiling, the Dictator sent Commander de Belveze of France to

Canada to represent him—and for the purpose of solidifying trade relations with Canada. The Commander's ship, *La Capricieuse*, flying the imperial colours of His Napoleonic Majesty, was the first French warship to come to Quebec after the conquest of Canada by the British.

In 1890, Quebec was visited by an ambassador-*ex-officio* of Napoleonic descent, Prince Roland Bonaparte. In the spring of 1948, His Royal Highness Prince Napoleon Louis Jerome, pretender to the throne of France, visited Quebec City. Assuming the name of Count Louis de Montfort, he remand incognito during his entire stay in the Château Frontenac. He is the son of Prince Victor Napoleon and Clementine, daughter of Leopold II of Belgium.

Chapter Fourteen

THE FIRST MENTION of a new hotel[1] for Quebec is found in Thomas J. Oliver's *Guide to Quebec,* published in 1882: "A company has lately been formed for the purpose of building a magnificent hotel on the vacant spot near the Terrace."

On April 18th, 1883, the French newspaper, *L'Evénement,* carried the following item (here translated):

> "The Hon. Messrs. Mousseau, Jean Blanchet and Lynch, visited yesterday morning the site of the projected grand hotel on the terrace. They were accompanied by the Hon. Mr. Garneau, one of the directors of the company, and Messrs. Willis Russell, John J. Foote, and others. The site was measured and the plans laid out, and it was decided that the border of eighteen feet of land which they wish to obtain from the government, will not affect the general appearance of the surroundings. It is believed that the Prime Minister has promised that the government will give every attention to the request of the Company."[2]

For the next eight years or so, Quebec teemed with rumours about this Company, who comprised it and when and where it proposed to build this wonderful hotel that was to excel anything ever built in Quebec or, indeed, anywhere in Canada. The citizens were considerably enlightened and encouraged when the following appeared in *The Canadian Gazette* of February 20th, 1890:

> "The necessary money having been subscribed, a meeting of the new hotel projectors has been held when it was decided to call the building the 'Fortress Hotel'. The following gentlemen were named the Provisional Directors, R. R. Dobell (one

[1]So far as the author could ascertain after considerable research.

[2]"Les hons. MM. Mousseau, Jean Blanchet, et Lynch, ont visité hier matin le site du grand hôtel projecté, sur la terrasse. Ils étaient accompagnés de l'hon. M. Garneau, un des directeurs de la compagnie, de MM. Willis Russell, John J. Foote et autres. On a mesuré et fait le tracé de l'emplacement, et l'on s'est convaincu que le lisière de dix pieds de terrain que l'on désire obtenir du gouvernement, ne nuira aucunement à l'apparance générale des environs. Le premier ministre aurait promis que le gouvernement donnerait tout son attention à la demande de la compagnie."

of the principal lumber shippers in Canada[3]); Hon. Thos. McGreevy, G. R. Renfrew, John Breakey, T. H. Dunn, Hon. G. Breese,[4] E. J. Hale."

The Quebec Daily Telegraph of February 21st, 1890, added this:

> "Mr. R. R. Dobell, accompanied by a leading architect, is visiting the principal cities of the United States in quest of the most suitable plan for the new Quebec hotel."

Again, on February 24th, the official *Gazette* of Quebec advised,

> "Public notice is hereby given, that within one month from the date of the last insertion of this notice, application will be made to His Honor, the Lieutenant Governor of this Province of Quebec, by the persons hereinafter named for Letters Patent under the great seal of the Province, constituting them a body politic, and corporate, under the provisions of the Joint Stock Company's Incorporation Act. The corporate name of the proposed Company will be 'The Fortress Hotel Company'."

Those applying for Letters Patent to form the Fortress Hotel Company were as follows: Timothy Hibbard Dunn, of the City of Quebec, merchant; Richard Reid Dobell, of the Parish of Sillery, merchant; George Richard Renfrew, of the City of Quebec, merchant; the Hon. Thomas McGreevy, member of the Parliament of Canada; the Hon. William Bresse, of the City of Quebec, Legislative Councillor of the Province; John Breakey, of the City of Quebec, merchant; Edward John Hale, of the City of Quebec, esquire; the Hon. George Irvine, of the City of Quebec, Queen's Counsel; Nicholas Karl Connolly, of the City of Quebec, contractor; Alphonse Charlebois, of the City of Quebec, contractor; James Boswell, of the City of Quebec, manufacturer; Veasey Boswell, of the City of Quebec, manufacturer.

And this was precisely what the citizens of Quebec had been trying to bring about: a hotel worthy of their growing city, a hotel that would afford accommodation not only for the occasional dignitaries who docked at the port of Quebec and for government officials during the sessions of the Provincial Legislature, but which

[3]Author's note re Mr. Dobell.
[4]This should read 'Hon. W. Bresse'.

would also encourage the world to beat a pathway to the city gates to see the treasures of history and the natural beauties it contained. The venture proposed by the Fortress Hotel Company had the whole-hearted sanction and the keen interest of government and municipal authorities.

The Fortress Hotel Company also entertained the idea that, as a hotel of the size contemplated might possibly not be feasible on the Terrace (near to the brow of the cliff, where once had stood the Château St. Louis) without the removal of the Château Haldimand, the site of the Montmorency-Laval Park was the next most suitable place for it. (This, as has been previously noted, was formerly the site of the Legislative Buildings). *The Daily Telegraph* of April 17th, 1890, further adds to the confusion as to where the hotel would be: "The plans for the new Fortress Hotel, to be erected on the old Parliament site, are now nearly ready, after which tenders will be called and building operations commenced."

Then some nine months later *The Canadian Gazette* advised its readers: "The capital subscribed so far for the Fortress Hotel amounts to 205,000 dollars, and the first call of ten percent has been met by all shareholders. Work will be commenced early in the spring. It is proposed to spend 175,000 dollars on the building."

Before long, however, the Fortress Hotel Company ran into difficulties, one of which was lack of money. A hotel such as they proposed to erect would, they discovered, cost more than $175,000 —whether it were on Dufferin Terrace or on the old Parliament site. Efforts were made to interest the Canadian Pacific Railway Company in the project but they were only successful in so far as they gained the support of certain officials of that Company who agreed to form another Company for the purpose of building a hotel. The Provincial Government and the City Fathers added their persuasions to induce the gentlemen in question to proceed with their plan, and the Company thereupon formed by Letters Patent dated July 16th, 1892, was known as the Château Frontenac Company, and consisted of the following distinguished persons: Sir Donald Alexander Smith, K.C.M.G.[5]; William Cornelius Van

[5]Lord Strathcona.

Horne[6], President, Canadian Pacific Railway Company; Richard Bladworth Angus, Director of the Canadian Pacific Railway; Thomas George Shaughnessy[7], Vice-President of the Canadian Pacific Railway; James Ross, contractor; all of Montreal; Edmund Boyd Osler, broker; Wilmot Deloui Matthews, grain merchant; both of Toronto; Sandford Fleming, civil engineer, Ottawa; William Hendrie, Hamilton.[8]

Messrs. Van Horne, Angus, Shaughnessy, Osler, and Ross were the directors of the newly formed Company, and it was but incidental at the time that several of these gentlemen were affiliated with the Canadian Pacific Railway Company.

On February 4th, 1892, *The Canadian Gazette* carried a most interesting item, quoted herewith in its entirety, which indicates that even at that late date there was some doubt as to just where this grand hotel would be located:

> "President Van Horne of the Canadian Pacific Railway, accompanied by R. B. Angus and E. B. Osler, have been here in connection with the scheme for the construction of a mammoth hotel in Quebec, which is to be ready for European travel *en route* to the World's Fair at Chicago, by 1st of May, 1893. Two architects accompanied the party, which visited the site of the old Parliament House, at the head of Mountain Hill, where the Fortress Hotel Company propose erecting a house, and also the property lately acquired on the cape by Lord Mount-Stephen, where the Canadian Pacific Railway at first thought of building. The visitors have decided the most favorable site would be on Government property adjoining Dufferin Terrace where the Normal School now stands. Subsequently at a meeting of shareholders of the Fortress Hotel Company held for the purpose of winding up the affairs of the Company, providing the Canadian Pacific Railway took hold of the scheme, Mr. Van Horne invited the shareholders to take stock in the new scheme, which was not a scheme of the C.P.R. but of several individual gentlemen, most of whom were connected with the Road. The local men undertook negotiations with the Government for the site. If obtained, work will commence in about six weeks."

[6]Later, Sir William Van Horne.
[7]Later, Sir Thomas Shaughnessy.
[8]Copied direct from Letters Patent, Parliament Buildings, Quebec City.

The capital of the new company was $300,000: twice the amount that the City Council of Quebec had stated the new hotel must cost. A Resolution of the Council, dated January 29th, 1892, stated, in effect, that any concern who would build a hotel within the walls of Upper Town, should disperse not less than $150,000, that the building should have not less than one hundred and fifty guest rooms, and that upon fulfilment of these requirements, such a concern would be allowed exemption from taxes for a period of ten years thereafter. For such a building to be tax-exempt for ten years, until it had had a chance to become a paying proposition, was not an inconsiderable matter, and any Company worthy of the name would hasten to avail themselves of such an advantage.[9]

Ultimately the Château Frontenac Company decided that the finest spot of all for such a hotel was atop the heights where once had stood the Château and Fort St. Louis, and where *still stood* the Château Haldimand.

Since this was progress at work in earnest, what had to be done was done: the Château Haldimand was *demolished.*

By March, 1892, the deed of land had been signed by Mr. Shaughnessy and Attorney-General T. C. Casgrain, and the contract with the Quebec Government for delivery of the site to the Château Frontenac Company had been put through. By April 21st, 1892, the Château Haldimand was but a pile of debris. This time the spirit of Sir Frederick Haldimand might have been hovering somewhere thereabout, frowning in rueful disapproval that his handiwork should thus be brought to such a pass. But then, Sir Frederick had been a progressive fellow and he probably understood the forces at work for the advancement of the city of Quebec.

The citizens of Quebec gathered around daily—as people will do when anything is being demolished or constructed—and one day they were amazed to see laid open to their view the solidly built rooms of the Ammunition Store, lately the offices of the Provincial Registrar, originally the old powder magazine. As these old walls were about to be razed, the people began to murmur. No one was quite sure of the history of this unquestionably ancient

[9]See *The Morning Chronicle's* Press Report, August 24th, 1893, of "Special Meeting of the City Council".

structure. And if it were, by chance, a last portion of the old Fort St. Louis, should it be destroyed?

The matter was somewhat clarified by Mr. J. M. Le Moine (later Sir James), noted historian and author, who wrote his opinions to the Editor of the local *Morning Chronicle* on March 21st, 1892:

> "To the Editor of the *Morning Chronicle,*
> Dear Sir:
>
> Those two vaulted rooms now laid bare in the rear of the Château Haldimand are exciting the curiosity of the crowds visiting this historic spot.
>
> What were they originally intended for: Are they much older than the main building, all are asking?
>
> My opinion, derived from old documents, is that they were magazines to store powder—they are detached from the old Château and the new Château sites. I am credibly informed that Mr. Van Horne or Mr. Shaughnessy, if appealed to in time, would try and preserve them as mementoes of the past and have them incorporated in some of the outer work of the new hotel.
>
> Won't somebody 'move' and try and preserve these relics, which would form quite an interesting study, for cultured tourists visiting Quebec?
>
> In an old plan now before me, of 1685—these two vaulted rooms are clearly indicated, as in process of construction; this would make them one hundred years older than the Château Haldimand.
>
> J. M. Le Moine
>
> Quebec, 21st March, 1892."

****

Thereupon, Mr. H. Y. Joly de Lotbinière took it upon himself to advise the Château Frontenac Company of the age and interest of these venerable walls, and sent them a copy of Mr. Le Moine's letter. No sooner had this information reached Mr. Van Horne and Mr. Shaughnessy than orders were issued that demolition on the walls be halted immediately and every effort made to have them incorporated into the new building. But the contractor, Mr. F. Labelle, wired Mr. Shaughnessy saying, "We are now ready to tear down the old vaulted rooms which I think could not be located in the new building, being pretty well torn down before orders were received not to do so." In a letter on the matter, Mr. Labelle is more explicit:

> "The walls are now getting dangerous, being weakened by the tearing down that has already been done to them. All the people here, with the exception of Mr. Le Moine and Mr. Joly (de Lotbinière) seem to be of the opinion that it would be far more preferable to pull them down than to have them built into the new building."

The Château Frontenac Company were now faced with the problem of endangering the foundation of their new building by using the old walls as part of the new (since the site of it was most necessary to their plans), or of offending the citizenry of Quebec by tearing down the old walls. Work came to a full stop until the Company at last decided that the portion of the walls which could be used without any possible or eventual danger to the building could be kept but the rest must be torn down. Fortunately no more was said by the citizens, so eager were they to have the hotel.

Early in May, 1892, work was begun on the foundation. Forty thousand cubic feet of solid rock had first to be displaced.

We can well imagine with what keen interest the people of Quebec watched the erection of the great hotel. Was it true that it would have over a hundred and fifty rooms? and that it was to be the same as a French château?

By the middle of 1892 it was generally assumed that the Canadian Pacific Railway Company had absorbed the Château Frontenac Company as a subsidiary, and from this time onward the new construction on Dufferin Terrace was referred to by the Press as "the new Canadian Pacific hotel", but as late as July, 1893, this was not officially true. From a letter written by Mr. W. C. Van Horne, dated July 3rd, 1893, is taken the following: "The Hotel at Quebec is not being built by the Canadian Pacific Railway Company, as is popularly supposed, but by individuals some of whom are connected with the Company and some are not."

Mr. Ernest Gagnon, (author of the book, *Fort et Château St. Louis*), who was at that time Secretary of the Department of

Public Works, was most interested in the new hotel. On September 1st, 1892, he took pen in hand and dropped a note to his good friend, Mr. W. J. Maguire, the Editor of *The Daily Mercury*, Quebec. This letter, which Mr. Maguire thoughtfully forwarded to Mr. Shaughnessy, said,

> "Would it not be interesting to have the *Arms* of the two French governors (Montmagny and Frontenac) on the big tower of the new hotel, one on each side of the *entrée d'honneur?*"[10]

Mr. Gagnon's suggestion was certainly carried out for today the crest of the House of Frontenac, from the Coat of Arms of the Comte de Palluau et Frontenac, carved in stone, can be seen over the entrance to the Château Frontenac, facing *Place d'Armes*. Montmagny's crest is, of course, the Malta Stone on the courtyard side of the entrance to the hotel.

The Frontenac crest consists of a shield of azure blue upon which are superimposed three golden griffin's paws with sharp talons; the crest is ensigned by the coronet of a French count, i.e., a coronet with nine pearls on its short golden spikes. In the Coat of Arms, on either side of the shield, are two winged griffins rampant, supporting it. The coronet is surmounted by a warrior's helmet which is guarded over by yet another griffin with wings outspread.

A griffin, according to William Cecil Wade's treatise on *The Symbolisms of Heraldry*, is "a chimerical creature (that) has the head, wings and talons of an eagle, and the body of a lion. . . . Guillim says that it 'sets forth the property of a valorous soldier whose magnanimity is such that he will dare all dangers, and even death itself rather than become captive.' It also symbolised Vigilancy . . ." Its purpose was to guard valuable treasures, among them the Pearl of Wisdom and the Jewel of Enlightenment, and its kinship was traced, in legend, to the Cherubim who guarded the Tree of Life in Paradise.

The Canadian Gazette of August 1st, 1893, reported: "The building of the Château Frontenac Hotel of the Canadian Pacific

[10]The tower to which Mr. Gagnon referred is the hexagonal tower of the Riverside Wing. The great Tower was not built until later.

Railway Company is being rapidly pushed forward, and the management hope that by October it will be so far advanced as to be open for the reception of guests. The correspondent here of the Toronto *Globe* says of this hotel that it is not to be excelled in appearance and ornamentation by any hotel on the continent."

The Château Frontenac Company were desirous of having title to the land (upon which the hotel was being constructed) "in perpetuity" but this was found impossible since the land was only leased to the Quebec Government by the Dominion Government for ninety-nine years. So the land was rented to them for a period of fifty years, at the rate of $1,250 per year, from the Quebec Government. When finally, some years later,[11] it was agreed that the land should be sold to the lessee, the sum paid was $25,000.

****

Who were these leading architects whom the Press kept referring to when reporting on the progress of the new hotel?

In the designing of the Château Frontenac, the Company employed the services of three famous architects and designers: Mr. Bruce Price of New York (who was the father of Emily Post of etiquette fame), and two brothers, Edward and William S. Maxwell of Montreal. Mr. Price was responsible for the structural design and exterior appointments; the Messrs. Maxwell looked after the interior decorating and the general design of each room, in particular the public spaces. Elegance and convenience; luxury and simplicity; ancient without, modern within; these were the keynotes of the Château Frontenac.

Thus it rose against the skyline of Quebec, to crown the height as it had never been crowned before even in the most affluent days of the old French régime! a building that was to be forever a thing of beauty looking down on beauty all around it. Incomparable structure in an incomparable setting!

[11]1941.

On the outer wall of the Château Frontenac there is a small plaque:

> Here stood the Chateau Haldimand,
> or Vieux Chateau, occupying part
> of outworks of the Fort St. Louis.
> Begun in 1784, completed in 1787,
> this edifice was displaced by the
> erection of the present Chateau
> Frontenac in 1892.

✻✻✻✻✻✻✻✻✻✻✻✻✻

APPENDIX FOR CHAPTER FOURTEEN

Excerpt from *Frontenac et Ses Amis,* by *Ernest Myrand,* p. 138

Sceau de Frontenac

"Frappé sur un 'Titre de concession, en date du 31 octobre, 1680, d'un lieue et demie au dessus du Sault, aux RR. P.P. de la Compagnie de Jésus à Québec'.

"Ce titre de concession est déposé aux Archives du Département des Terres, Mines et Pêcheries de la Province de Québec. Il a été gracieusement communiqué à l'auteur par M. Eugène-Etienne Taché, sous-ministre du Département.

"Les armes et le sceau de Frontenac, ainsi que les armes de Montmort sont reproduits d'après les dessins de M. Eugène Hamel, artiste, officier du service civil.

"Les photogravures de ces dessins ont été exécutées aux ateliers de la maison Binner Engraving Company, de Chicago."

Armes de Montmort

"D'Azur, au chevron d'or, accompagné de trois anilles d'argent."

The *Dictionnaire de la Noblesse,* par de la Chenaye-Desbois et Badier (1864) gives the coat of arms of the County of Buade in the Province of Touraine, France, as: "d'azur, à trois pattes de griffon d'or, posées 2 and 1".

Chapter Fifteen

"BEYOND THE SHADOW of a doubt, the finest hotel site in the world is that now occupied by the Château Frontenac of this city, which today throws open its doors for the first time, for the reception of guests. It rises in all its stately grandeur upon the very margin of Dufferin Terrace—that incomparable promenade which is the pride of Quebec. Of this Terrace it has been written that 'there is not such another in the whole world'.

"In form the building is something like a horseshoe, the space in the centre being occupied by a large courtyard, measuring 170 by 100 feet. This space is paved in cement, and in the centre there will be a fountain. The main entrance is found in this court, which is reached through a handsome arch of stone, supported by colonnades of the same material. The exterior of the archway faces St. Louis street and is surmounted by the historic keystone bearing a Maltese Cross and the date of 1647. . . . The principal material used in the construction of the walls is a handsome fire brick, which was brought from Scotland specially for the purpose. The foundation wall and the pretty and graceful cornices, the turrets and the upper parts of the round and hexagonal towers are built of a rich grey stone from the quarries of Lachevrotière. The roofing throughout is of copper, which harmonizes very prettily with the colour of the brick. . . . The turrets and towers lend to the whole structure the appearance of a mediaeval castle perched upon a precipice. On Des Carrières street the building's frontage is 283 feet, opposite to the Place d'Armes 70 feet, facing the Post Office 100 feet, and towards the Terrace 120 feet. This variety in the different directions in which the building fronts affords a view, the range of which extends from the Citadel to Lorette if seen from the upper stories, and to Beauport as seen from below. From the extremity of the wing facing on to Des Carrières street to the extremity of that over-looking the Terrace the distance is 120 feet.

"Once in the vestibule the visitor is at once struck with the beauty of the mosaic stone flooring and the richness of the woodwork and mural decorations. The carved oaken mouldings and dentil cornices are very elaborate and beautiful. Upon the walls are a variety of inlaid tapestries. Facing the guest as he approaches the foot of the grand staircase are the arms of Frontenac, and these, painted upon his shield and supported by Knights in sixteenth century armor, are repeated over the ticket office and news stand. Frontenac and Montmagny are each represented in complete armor, bearing their arms and shields, and the arms of the Province are surmounted in some cases with the names of distinguished Viceroys, including those of Champlain and Sherbrooke in addition to those already mentioned. There are also the arms of the Dominion and the Province, in some cases supported by griffins, and the dates, '1608-1893', marking, of course, the epochs of the founding of Quebec and of the erection of the hotel, or more correctly speaking, perhaps, at all events so far as the intentions of the designer are concerned, if not chronologically, those of the construction of the two Châteaux upon very nearly the same site.[1]

"The Coffee Room is a spacious apartment on the first floor,[2] occupying the extremity of the wing that stretches towards St. Louis street. As in the case of the dining room, which is immediately above it, the windows on the south side look across the courtyard and over the Terrace and garden in the direction of the Citadel, and on the north side overlook the Post Office and the Place d'Armes. Its dimensions are almost those of the dining room, which measures 58 feet by 45, the only difference in size being that one of the corners of the Coffee Room has been cut off. The furnishings of the room consist of a variety of oaken tables and chairs. . . . Over the large open fireplace, which is of Tennessee marble, is the motto from the crest of the city of Quebec: '*Natura Fortis, Industria Crescit*'. The walls are a rich brown colour, with illuminated frieze below the cornices, and oak wainscotting.

"The dining room is situated in the Place d'Armes extension of the Château, on the second floor,[3] immediately above the

[1]1608 was the date of the founding of the city of Quebec, but the first château was not built until 1647, by Governor Montmagny. Champlain failed in his attempt to build it in 1620-24.

[2]Meaning the ground floor. This room is now the Jacques Cartier Room. The bar was, at that time, on the basement floor, in what is now the Ski Room.

[3]This is considered the first floor.

Coffee Room. It has a breakfast room in the hexagonal tower as an annex. . . . The floors are of oak in herring-bone pattern. But the most attractive features of the dining room itself are the magnificent views from the windows and the rare and beautiful tapestries that decorate the walls and are inserted all around them within the oaken-framed panels. These tapestries represent the history of the foundation of Rome.[4] They are equally of interest because they represent an important event in the history of the Roman Empire, and because the characters depicted are costumed after the fashion of the sixteenth century, the epoch of the architecture of the Château. The treatment of the room, in keeping with the character of the whole building, is exactly what would have been executed at the epoch referred to, excepting, of course, that up to the end of the seventeenth century, tapestries were only hung upon rings on the walls and never fastened, for the reason that nobles, copying the customs of the kings, travelled from castle to castle with their tapestries, which, together with their trophies of war, were the only ornaments of the stone walls.

"The Ladies Parlour[5] is a circular room in the circular tower on the second floor. The woodwork is of white mahogany and the fireplaces are of handsome Jaune Lamartine marble, lined with soapstone . . . the floor is carpeted in first quality Axminsters.[6] The furniture is partly in brocade, partly in corduroy, to match the delicate tints of the walls.

"The hotel contains no less than 170 bedrooms, 93 of which are supplied with bathrooms.[7] All have wardrobes and open fireplaces, the grates being surrounded with Minton tiles of various

[4]Carrel's illustrated *Guide and Map of Quebec* (16th Edit. 1908) says: "The tapestries that surround the dining room of the Chateau Frontenac consist of a repetition of five panels composing the 'Foundation of Rome' series, the original of which is in the Royal Palace at Madrid. In the first panel are to be seen Romulus and Remus, being suckled by a she-wolf and discovered by Faustulus. After the death of Numa, King of Alba, Romulus was enthroned and founded Rome, and these incidents are depicted on panel number two. The third panel is a representation of the bringing of Hersilia before Romulus after the rape of the Sabines. In the fourth panel, Romulus is shown in the act of administering law to the people, appointing lictors, etc. An intricate scene illustrative of the prosperity of Rome in the palmy days of her greatness, forms the subject of the fifth panel of the series."

[5]Now known as the Rose Room—on the first floor.

[6]Fire destroyed these properties in 1926.

[7]Today the hotel has been expanded, by the addition of wings, until it has four times as many bedrooms as in 1893.

shades. The washstands and fixtures are of solid marble. The bedrooms are of various shapes: square, triangular, fan-shaped, oval. . . . The furniture is all of oak in the sixteenth century style,[8] the carpets are all Miltons.[9]

"The architect, Mr. Bruce Price, of New York, has every reason to feel proud of his work in connection with the Château Frontenac, and so has Mr. Felix Labelle, who built the entire structure for the Company.

"The Manager of the Château Frontenac is H. S. Dunning, Esq., one of the most successful and most experienced hotel men in America.[10] As his heads of departments, Mr. Dunning has selected the following: Chief Clerk—Mr. Frank Stanton, late of the Queen's, Toronto; Second Clerk—Mr. Nelson de Quetteville, who is already well and favourably known in Quebec; Night Clerk—Mr. John Brennan, the late successful manager of the St. Lawrence Hotel, Cacouna; Chef—Mr. Henry E. Journet; between 1871 and 1875 he (Mr. Journet) was at the Maison Dorée, Paris, the Grand Hotel, and at the Elysée with President MacMahon; subsequently, he went to the Devonshire Club, London, and the Star and Garter, and afterwards entered the service of the Prince Royal Alexander of Holland; latterly, he has been with Secretary Whitney at New York; Housekeeper—Mrs. Newkirk, who has occupied a similar position in several leading hotels in New York; Chief Barkeeper—Mr. George Haas."

The foregoing was the report carried by *The Quebec Morning Chronicle* on December 18th, 1893, the day the Château Frontenac opened for business. Regarding the first guests the *Chronicle* continued, "a distinguished party of Montreal gentlemen got ahead of the Château Frontenac last night by registering there and securing quarters a day ahead of the formal opening. Amongst them are Messrs. Angus Hooper, R. MacD. Paterson, W. F. Angus, John Taylor and Ald. Préfontaine, M.P.P."

Upon reading the foregoing excerpts from the Press it should be borne in mind that, like many such large buildings consisting of

[8]Since replaced to some extent, for greater comfort.
[9]Time and many feet have brought replacement.
[10]The *Chronicle* of March 16th, 1893, in its column "City and District Items", advises that Mr. Dunning was formerly of the Windsor Hotel in Montreal.

many wings, the Château Frontenac's wings were added at different times, and that the description here reported is only applicable to the portion now known as the Riverview Wing which, in 1893, comprised the entire building. In 1899 the Citadel Wing and Citadel Pavilion were added, extending the Château along Mont Carmel street; in 1909 the Mont Carmel Wing continued the building along the same street; the St. Louis Wing, facing the Mont Carmel Wing, was built in 1921; and the great Tower, which dominates the whole, was erected in 1920-1924, together with the service wing which connects the Mont Carmel and St. Louis wings and forms the circular courtyard as it is today.[11] The Tower was the crowning note, the climax of the whole building, bearing in appearance the same relationship to the other wings as the control tower of many mediaeval châteaux of France. It had seventeen stories, sixteen of which were guest floors, averaging seventeen rooms on each.[12]

The facts of construction of this masterpiece of architecture are really worth more than a cursory glance. The entire building was constructed in accordance with the best engineering practice as to fireproofing; a heavy skeleton of steel was wrapped with metal fabric and fireproofed with stone concrete, with reinforced concrete floor and roof slabs; interior partitions were of terra cotta, except around the stairs, halls, elevators, and fire escapes where gypsum blocks were used; heavy and substantial exterior walls were of brick trimmed with stone, all laid up in cement mortar. The roof consisted of structural steel rafters, on which was laid reinforced metal lath, plastered with a composition of sand, Portland cement and asbestos[31].

Of the twenty suites in the Château Frontenac, sixteen are in the tower and four are in the Riverview Wing. The Tower suites are furnished with infinite care, having regard for beauty, comfort and good taste, after the manner of the châteaux of France, the mansion houses of England—and a little of old Holland for variety. Then, there are the now famous Crown Suites, so named after Royalty from England were guests there in May, 1939. The

[11]See sketch supplied by the Canadian Pacific Railway Company.
[12]From sidewalk to top of Tower, the Château Frontenac is 251 feet 6 inches.
[13]Details supplied by the Canadian Pacific Railway Company.

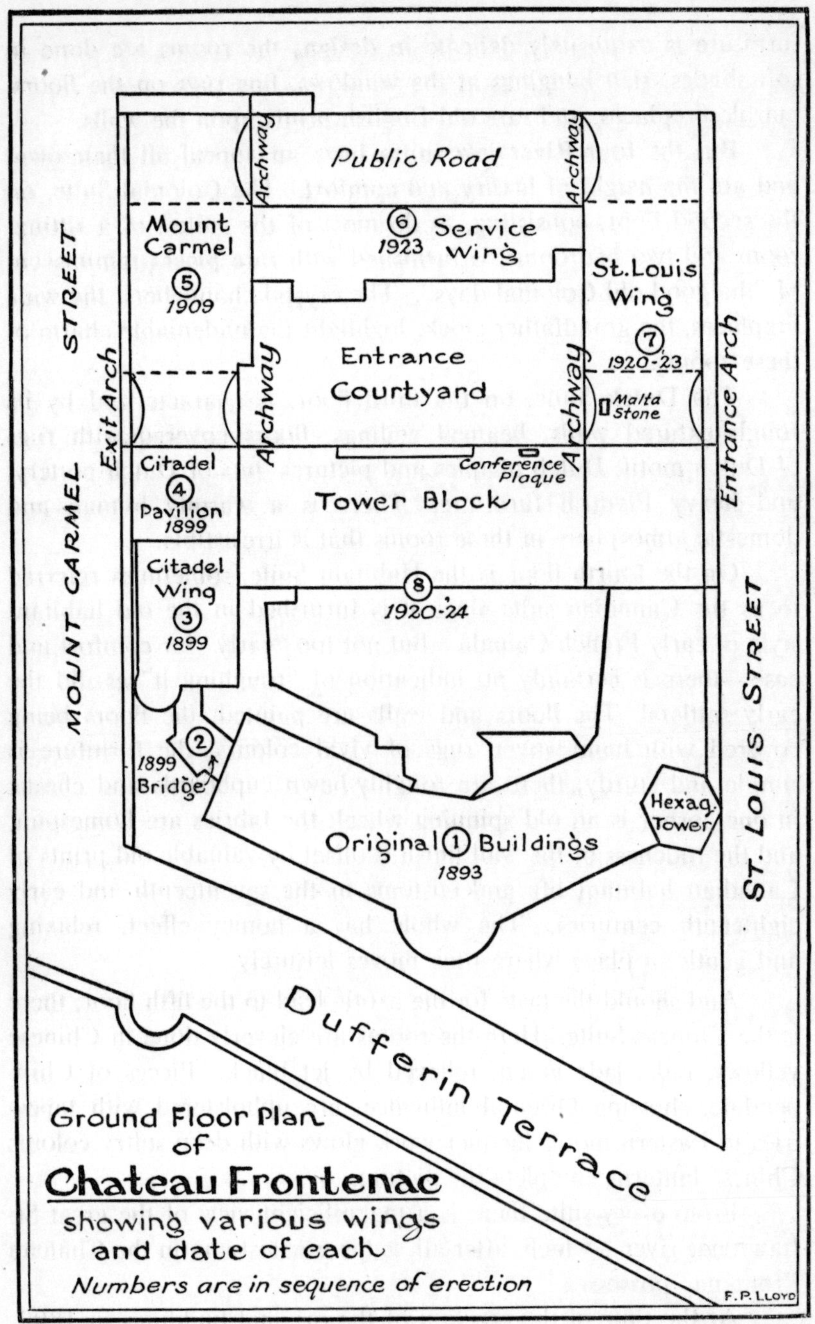
Public Road
Archway
Archway
Mount Carmel
5
1909
6
1923
Service Wing
St. Louis Wing
7
1920-23
MOUNT CARMEL STREET
Exit Arch
Archway
Entrance Courtyard
Archway
Malta Stone
Entrance Arch
Citadel Pavilion
4
1899
Conference Plaque
Tower Block
Citadel Wing
3
1899
8
1920-24
ST. LOUIS STREET
2
1899
Bridge
Hexag. Tower
Original 1 Buildings
1893
Dufferin Terrace
Ground Floor Plan of
Chateau Frontenac
showing various wings and date of each
Numbers are in sequence of erection
F. P. LLOYD

furniture is exquisitely delicate in design; the rooms are done in soft shades, rich hangings at the windows, fine rugs on the floors, marble fireplaces, and rare old English prints upon the walls.

But the four Riverview suites have an appeal all their own, and are the height of luxury and comfort. The Colonial Suite, on the second floor, consisting, as do most of the suites, of a sitting-room and two bedrooms, is furnished with rare pieces reminiscent of "the good old Colonial days". The crystal chandeliers, the wide fireplaces, the grandfather clock, highlight the undeniable charm of these rooms.

The Dutch Suite, on the third floor, is characterized by its rough-textured walls, beamed ceilings, floors covered with rugs of Dutch motif, Dutch plaques and pictures, bits of Dutch pottery, and heavy Flemish furniture. There is a warmly human and domestic atmosphere in these rooms that is irresistible.

On the fourth floor is the Habitant Suite, sometimes referred to as the Canadian suite since it is furnished in the old habitant style of early French Canada—but not too "early" for comfort and ease—there is certainly no indication of "roughing it" as did the early settlers! The floors and walls are painted, the floors being covered with hand-woven rugs of vivid colours; the furniture is simple and sturdy; there are roughly-hewn cupboards and chests; in one corner is an old spinning wheel; the fabrics are homespun; and the rudeness of the wall finish is offset by valuable old prints of Canadian habitant life and customs in the seventeenth and early eighteenth centuries. The whole has a homey effect, relaxing and gentle, a place where time moves leisurely.

And should the taste for the exotic lead to the fifth floor, there is the Chinese Suite. Here the rooms are cleverly done in Chinese yellows, reds, jade green, relieved by jet black. Pieces of Chippendale, showing Oriental influence, are upholstered with tapestries in Eastern motif, lacquer work glows with deep sultry colour; Chinese lanterns complete the picture.

From every suite there is a magnificient view of the great St. Lawrence river—which, after all, is the greatest charm the Château Frontenac possesses.

At the time of the erection of the original buildings in 1892-

1893, and for many years thereafter until the building was completed as it now stands, the furniture for the Château Frontenac was chosen with minutest care. When the Tower suites were being furnished in 1924, the firm of architects, Edward and W. S. Maxwell of Montreal, who had designed the tower in accordance with the design of Bruce Price's original building, sent a special commissioner to England and France, at the behest of the Canadian Pacific Railway Company, in a search for genuine antiques, and to make arrangements for the finest of copies to be made of such originals as were not for sale. On this mission Mr. Edward Maxwell visited seventeen cathedral towns in England and almost as many in France. While in Paris he dealt with a firm which was, at that time, the only one in France allowed to remove pieces from the national Museums for reproduction purposes. This was arranged for Mr. Maxwell through the good offices of the great French architect, Violett-le-Duc, then Director-General of Historical Monuments for the French Government.

The lists of furniture purchased by Mr. Maxwell on this trip in 1922 are impressive. Jacobean oak bedsteads . . . Chippendale mahogany bureaux and grandfather chairs . . . Sheraton mahogany cupboard . . . Queen Anne walnut writing table and candle stands . . . Adam rosewood and tulipwood tables . . . Dutch tortoise-shell mirror and inlaid chair . . . Louis XV gilt bronze mirror frames . . . Louis XIV oak dressing tables . . . Charles II oak day bed . . . Cromwellian armchair . . . Italian carved mirrors . . . And each piece, as well as dozens of others, had its accompanying ensemble to furnish a room or suite of rooms.

Of course, today this fine old furniture has suffered from the wear of time and people—many of whom—alas!—did not realize what they damaged. Consequently, much has had to be replaced—and quickly—at times when similar pieces were not obtainable at any price.

It has been said that the Château Frontenac has more public space than any other hotel on the North American continent. The interior of the building is designed in such a distinctive manner as to be equally as fascinating as the exterior. The shape of the lobby is that of a "T"—the two top "arms" extend to the right and left of the main entrance; the "leg" of the "T" is known as the Grande Allée which extends from the entrance to the river front, culminating in the St. Lawrence Room[14] which overlooks Dufferin Terrace and the river. At the left of the main entrance, at the end of the "arm" of the "T", is one of the Grand Staircases of the hotel; this one goes up to the Salon de Verchères, the ballroom and the dining-room. It is a twin stairway of Villarville marble, sweeping in gracious curves to meet at the entrance to the Salon de Verchères on the floor above. It is said to have been inspired by a similar staircase in the Petit Trianon of Versailles, which was one of the abodes of Marie Antoinette when she was Queen of France. The walls of the stairway are of Rippe-Doré marble, imported from France. The balustrades are of delicate wrought-iron, the newels are of bronze cast by the Cire Perdu process, the handrails are of solid extruded bronze, a material that permitted the curves to be formed with practically no use of cast work. Midway along the Grande Allée is the second Grand Staircase of marble, similar to the first.

The lobby floor is of the same marble as the stairs, and is covered with large Khorasan rugs. The walls are panelled in quartered oak of a neutral brown colour. The ceiling features wide beams and mural decorations of painted polychrome, based on sixteenth century figures, done by the famous muralist, Smeraldi. The windows are tall, deep-set, small-paned, with a small brilliant stained-glass medallion in each depicting ships of the early discoverers of Canada.

At the foot of the first Grand Staircase is a splendid statue of General James Wolfe, which is a replica of the original at Greenwich, England, birthplace of the General. It was executed by the well-known Canadian sculptor, Dr. Tait McKenzie, "moulder of clay and of men". The long flowing cloak, the telescope in his right hand for scanning the heights he must scale to take Quebec, the forward-thrust head with thoughtful face, left hand at his hip— all are said to be truly characteristic of the General, and all have been faithfully reproduced by the late Dr. McKenzie.

The Jacques Cartier Room[15] overlooking Place d'Armes square

[14]The writing room.
[15]For dancing.

is quite unique, its theme being a representation, as nearly as possible, of the interior of the cabin of the great explorer, Jacques Cartier, on his ship the *Grande Hermine,* in which he discovered *la Nouvelle France* in 1534. Three arches at its entrance are of specially-processed Kato stone; the deep fireplace is of the same stone, the mantel of which has a carved and polychromed frieze of oak, with motifs of early sixteenth century France; on the mantel is a model of the *Grande Hermine.* Small buffets with plate racks flank the fireplace giving the room an intimate character. The room is low-ceilinged with beams of rich brown fumed oak, and the walls are oak-panelled; lighting fixtures are ship's lanterns in wrought iron, and the chandeliers carry out a nautical motif; the windows are metal casements of leaded squares which open outwards, and in the centre of each casement is a jewel-like stained-glass depiction of figures of Canadian history. Several excellent reproductions of famous paintings grace the walls, among them those of the Comte and Comtesse de Frontenac.

The Champlain Room (also on the main floor—through which the Jacques Cartier Room is reached) is a long and restful lounge overlooking the Terrace. Here is found the largest fireplace in the Château, surrounded by deep divans and armchairs, where a sixteenth-century orchestra (complete with costumes) plays soft music to blend with the subdued sound of silver spoons against china teacups.

The Salon de Verchères is a rich and palatial sitting-room, not large, floored in marble, with low arches and columns, the ceiling decorated in leaves and flowers of green tones into which are introduced graceful scroll designs and cameo motifs. Plants and ferns carry out the soft colour scheme, and at twin points in the length of the room are marble well-heads for flowers and plants; bowls of metal, with four legs after the fashion of Greek and Roman braziers, hold electric lamps concealed to give the room a mysterious glow.

The gold and blue Ballroom is said to be a replica of the Hall of Mirrors at Versailles, with the exception of windows instead of mirrors, and the appointments are in Louis XV style. The upper walls and ceiling are elegantly carved; the stage, at one end, is faced by a balcony at the other which has an exquisite wrought-iron railing. Lighting is from bronze doré wall sconces of blue and mirror glass, and from crystal chandeliers which were imported especially for the room.

****

Is it possible that the interior of a building such as the Château Frontenac, requiring good taste and judgment in its décor, as well as consideration for comfort and practicability, could have been accomplished without the hand of a woman?—It might have been, but it wasn't.

Too few women have been featured in this long tale of the châteaux of Quebec, and those few were chiefly of the French régime. But now we come to a woman of the British régime, a woman of such beauty of face and stature, of such warm charm and personality, that she could never pass unnoticed wherever she moved. At the time of her sojourn in the Château Frontenac she was Mrs. Hayter Reed, wife of the Manager of the Château, but she had been born Kate Armour, eldest daughter of the Honourable John Douglas Armour, Toronto, a Judge of the Supreme Court of Canada. It was once said of Kate Reed that "no other woman in Canada can surpass her either in knowledge of literature or affairs, or as an interesting and engaging conversationalist".[16]

Mr. Reed was manager of the hotel from 1900 to 1905, when he was made Director of Hotels for the Canadian Pacific Railway Company, a post he held until his retirement in 1915. During their stay in Quebec in the early nineteen hundreds, Mrs. Reed moved about the great modern castle, which was their home, with an artistic eye upon all its furnishings. Here was a woman who loved fine things, whose taste had been nurtured by years of study of furniture, brasses, copper, tapestries, paintings . . . and here was a wide field in which her talent could shine . . . Because of the delightful results she obtained in the Château Frontenac, the Canadian Pacific Hotel System soon realized the value of Mrs. Reed's artistry, and when Mr. Reed was made Director of Hotels, Mrs. Reed, accompanying him on his business visits across Canada,

[16]Mrs. George Cran, *A Woman in Canada,* (1910).

was in consultation with the architects in the decoration of nearly all of their hotels.

Mrs. Reed kept an extensive furniture diary. In it there is the following remarkable observation,

"It is through its power to give back the past and the quickening touch it lays on memory, recalling a sentiment here, a tragedy there, that makes furniture command our interest and our affection—for I am sure we leave our impressions on inanimate objects—we endow them with some of our own personality."

The decorations of the Château Frontenac "command our interest"; they have been endowed with the personality of such a woman as Mrs. Hayter Reed.

Mrs. Reed died in England in 1928, at the age of seventy-two.

****

The first function of note held in the Château Frontenac after its official opening took place on the evening of December 28th, 1893, when a certain Miss Gladys White made her début at a ball given in her honour by Lieutenant-General and Mrs. Wilson of Quebec. Assuredly on that night the Château Frontenac came to full bloom, its lights blazingly reflected in the great St. Lawrence, in a setting like a Christmas card, snow and frost creating a winter fairyland, rimming the eaves of the turrets and the sloping roofs. Inside, all was music, laughter, brilliance; colourful gowns, a sprinkling of military uniforms, good food and dancing.

Supper, served at midnight, was a lavish display of food: *bouillon, hors-d'oeuvres, entrée, salades, plats ornés* (beef, chicken, ham), *rôtis* (chicken, partridge), *entremets sucrés*, fruits, *glacés, thé, café*. Then, like the predecessors of both English and French, the guests rose from feasting and danced well into the night. . . .

An interesting sidelight on the evening's musical programme was the playing of a brilliant piece of music, well adapted for dancing, called the *Château Frontenac Quadrille*. It had been composed by a local music teacher of Quebec, Mrs. R. Jacques.

****

Chapter Sixteen

THE DATE, JANUARY 16th, 1926, escaped by a narrow margin from being a second January 23rd, 1834. The Château Frontenac almost met the fate of the Château St. Louis!

Fire broke out about twilight—on a day bitterly and icily similar to that other January day—in the Riverside Wing, on its fifth floor. In very short order the fire had done damage to the extent of seven hundred and sixty thousand dollars. Exactly the same winter conditions prevailed as in the disaster of 1834; the same cold wind and sub-zero temperature — but fortunately for the Château Frontenac, the fire-fighting apparatus was in excellent condition and even though water froze as it struck the building the equipment was kept in working order. But soon the lovely Castle of Quebec was a mass of blackened icicles—an ice palace of distorted proportion and grotesque decoration.

No one had been hurt, nor even endangered; and when the ice had melted it was found that only a portion of the building had been damaged; most of the valuable furniture, tapestries and paintings had been removed with a minimum of destruction.

Discouraging indeed to those who had spent so much time and money on this building. Nevertheless, advantage was taken of the disaster to rebuild the wing finer than before, equipping it with facilities more modern than those which had been available in 1893, replacing lost furniture with some of equal quality and beauty, retaining in the rooms the same successful colour schemes that had been chosen so carefully by Mrs. Hayter Reed. In exterior appearance as well as design, the wing was as nearly as possible exactly as before, for the builders were fortunate enough to obtain Bruce Price's original plans for that section.

No less than twelve hundred men swarmed at one time upon this construction in the work of restoration. And it was finished, ready for use, in one hundred and twenty-seven working days! It was opened to the public again on June 1st, of the same year in which it had been damaged—a monument to Canadian energy, will power and workmanship.

****

After the fire the Château Frontenac's career was more or less uneventful except for the increasing number of notables and celebrities from all over the world who came to visit it. Less than fifty years had passed over the new-old building before the register carried such distinguished names as the Earl and Countess of Aberdeen, the Earl and Countess Gray, the Duke and Duchess of Connaught, Lord and Lady Willingdon, Lord and Lady Bessborough, Lord and Lady Tweedsmuir, the Earl of Athlone and Princess Alice; (the gentlemen were in turn Governors-General of Canada).

Then there were the late Duke of Kent, the Dukes of Devonshire and Gloucester, the King and Queen of Siam, Princess Juliana of the Netherlands, Princess Alexandra Kropotkin, Sir Douglas Haig, Baron Byng (of Vimy), Earl Jellicoe (of Jutland), Lord Halifax, the Honourable Stanley Baldwin, the Honourable Ramsay MacDonald, Admiral Byrd, Madame Chiang Kai Chek, Marshal Ferdinand Foch, Marshal Fayolle, Colonel Charles Lindberg, Mr. Theodore Roosevelt. There were the screen stars, Jeannette MacDonald, Lily Pons, Walter Pidgeon, Barbara Stanwyck, Glenn Ford, Grace Moore, Don Ameche, Joan Bennett, Monty Woolley, Ramon Navarro, Ann Harding, Conrad Veidt, Douglas Fairbanks Sr., Raymond Massey, Louise Fazenda, Boris Karloff, Ben Turpin, Barbara Lamarr, Nancy Carrol, as well as Paul Whiteman, Alfred Lunt and Lynn Fontanne of Broadway. The great fighters of the world were there, too, at one time or another: Jack Sharkey, Gene Tunney, Jack Dempsey. . . .

Canada's own great politician, Sir Wilfrid Laurier, was first registered in the Château Frontenac on January 3rd, 1894, when he and his wife were listed as *M. et Mme.* Laurier, Arthabaska, Sir Wilfrid's constituency.

The year 1939 is invariably referred to as the "Year of the Royal Visit". On the seventeenth of May of that year, King George VI and Queen Elizabeth arrived at Quebec aboard the white liner, Empress of Australia. Once again Quebec was made gay with decorations to welcome Royalty to Canadian shores. The Castle of Quebec was draped with bunting and flags and gloriously floodlit at night; Dufferin Terrace was festooned with lights and flags; thousands of visitors flocked to the old city to help its citizens welcome the Sovereigns to Canada. The heights were lined with people who had equipped themselves with binoculars, opera glasses, cameras—and lunch boxes.

Amid all the pageantry which tradition decrees should accompany this charmingly natural couple, the King and Queen disembarked at Wolfe's Cove on that misty May morning to begin a triumphant tour that has never been equalled. They had been due in Quebec two days previously but, having encountered fog conditions at sea, were two days behind schedule; consequently the visit to Quebec, for which two days had been allotted, was cut in half—allowing very little time for visiting the birthplace of Canada.

The Château Frontenac was in its glory. For just such occasions it had been built. For just such visitors, so familiar with elegance, had it been designed and decorated! And yet, as soon as word was received that Royal visitors were coming, the great building underwent an immense preparation. Everything that was clean was cleaned again; everything that shone was polished again; every neat suit was pressed again. The finest furniture, carpets, draperies, were assembled for the suites which would be occupied by the Royal pair and their entourage; the finest floral decorations were ordered; the best silverware was re-polished, and the rules governing decorations for Royal occasions, the proper use of the Royal Standard, Coat of Arms and replicas of the Crown, were reviewed and rigidly followed.

Two splendid functions were tendered Their Majesties in the Château: the Canadian Government's luncheon, and the Provincial Government's banquet. The menus were masterpieces of good food and elegance featuring French-Canadian *cuisine*:

LUNCHEON

Le Melon Cantaloup Frappé
Les Queues de Homard Frontenac
La Poitrine de Poussin Grillée
Le Soufflé Glacé Grand Marnier
Les Petits Fours

La Corbeille de Fruits
Le Café

BANQUET

Les Perles des Sterlet
Le Consommé de Volaille Montmorency
Les Truites des Laurentides au Vin Blanc
La Couronne d'Agneau de Québec aux Primeurs
Le Sorbet au Champagne
Les Petits Oiseaux Blancs de l'Isle d'Orleans en Belle Vue
La Salade Gauloise
La Coupe Fraises Chantilly
Les Friandises
La Corbeille de Fruits

The luncheon in the Château Frontenac was the first meal that King George and Queen Elizabeth ate in Canada, and it was obvious that they enjoyed it. The Queen graciously complimented the Manager of the Château,[1] saying, with the pleasant smile so characteristic of her, "The flowers were lovely. The hotel is delightful and the food delicious; you have a good chef."[2]

The years were light and gentle with the castle of Quebec from 1927 to the autumn of 1939. But then European affairs were moving toward the inevitable turmoil. The King and Queen of England had scarcely been at home three months when Great Britain declared war on Germany, to be followed by Canada and the other dominions of the Empire. Once more dark and gloomy colours were woven into the tapestry of Quebec, showing up the brilliance of past years.

As in the wars of the past, the French in Canada were not wholly in accord with Great Britain in this one. There were many among them who, considering it "England's war", refused at first to become involved. No one, it seemed, remembered the famous words of Sir Wilfrid Laurier, "We are faithful to the great nation that gave us life (France); we are faithful to the great nation that gave us liberty (England)." But when it became apparent that the fate of the world was at stake, that no corner of the world would

[1]Then, Mr. B. A. Neale; now Mr. G. J. Jessop, who succeeded Mr. Neale in 1945.
[2]Mr. Louis Baltera.

remain untouched by the bloody holocaust, that the world would eventually fall under German domination unless all the world combined to prevent it, Quebec fell in line and, before the victorious end in 1945, had chalked up an estimable record.

Quebec City's war record is distinguished beyond question by the two great War Conferences that were held within its walls in 1943 and 1944. And thus was the Château Frontenac afforded another opportunity to play an important part in the history of the City and, this time, in the history of the world.

It all began—so far as the castle of Quebec is concerned—on July 31st, 1943, when the Canadian Government notified the Management that it would require the building for war purposes on August 8th for a period of two weeks or longer. This was followed by orders that all guests must vacate the hotel not later than August 6th, that no staff should remain after that date unless possessed of special passes issued by the Royal Canadian Mounted Police, and that no one should enter the building or its premises without the identification card issued for that purpose.

Among the thousands of details that had to be attended to without a moment's delay was the converting of the entire third floor—one hundred and one rooms—into offices. It had been decided that this would be the core of the deliberations of the Chiefs of Staff and delegates. No one was to have access to this "holy of holies" unless possessed of the rare and almost unobtainable "Blue Pass". The only rooms left undisturbed on this floor were those of the manager's personal suite—and when his laundry was brought to him, the page boy was escorted by two Royal Marines!

It soon became obvious to those immediately concerned with these fantastic arrangements that this augured another Council of War such as had been held at Casablanca and in mid-Atlantic, but everything was kept so secret that all the public could do (including those eight hundred and forty-nine guests who were asked to leave the hotel with no excuses proffered, and the two or three thousand people who were notified that their confirmed reservations were cancelled) was surmise and conjecture. Quebec seethed with speculation. Rumours flew wildly. One reported that the Château Frontenac was to become a hospital for wounded from the Sicilian battlefront. Another, that the Pope was to transform it into a second Vatican until the war should be over. But those who knew were silent.

Inside the Château Frontenac there was such activity as not even the Château St. Louis had witnessed in all its hundred and eighty-seven years of history-watching. Not a single department of the hotel was undisturbed by the transformation. All the offices of the delegations had to be specially wired for secret communicating apparatus, and for wire-photo transmitting and receiving sets. A complete private switchboard was installed and a special directory issued for the guests; many of its pages might have been taken from Burke's *Peerage* or *Who's Who.* The American delegates were assigned quarters on the "even-number" floors from the 16th floor down; the British had the "odd-numbers"; the fourth floor was held for Canadian Government officials.

The activities of everyone connected with the Conference were regulated by special Passes. A pink Pass admitted the bearer to the hotel but not to the third floor conference rooms; a blue Pass admitted the bearer to the hotel, including the sacred third floor; a buff Pass was admittance to the Citadel but not to the official Residence there; a white Pass (very restricted!) was for the Citadel *and* the Residence *and* the hotel; a white Surcharged Residence Staff Pass admitted the bearer to the Citadel and Residence, but not to the hotel.

When all was ready, the great of the world began to arrive in Quebec. Perhaps, after all the furore of planning and preparation, the Château Frontenac was a little disappointed that the greatest of Quebec's visitors on this historic occasion—the President of the United States, Franklin D. Roosevelt; the Prime Minister of Great Britain, Winston S. Churchill; the Prime Minister of Canada, William L. Mackenzie King—did not stay under its hospitable roof. But perhaps in these danger-fraught days when war was breaking out anew in unexpected places, a stone building was considered not safe enough for these key men, even though it was surrounded by anti-aircraft guns, alive with Army and Navy personnel; not safe enough for the highly secret deliberations that were to take place when the Three put their heads together to see how best the war could be won. But there was a safer place in Quebec than the Château Frontenac: the Citadel.

Surrounded by high stone walls, with gates of thick iron chain, teeming with soldiers, bristling with guns trained on the river on three sides and sweeping the sky from all angles, and set in a land far from the centre of war where enemy bombs had never fallen, the Citadel was assuredly one of the safest places in the world at that time—thanks to the Duke of Wellington who, in 1823, had caused it to be rebuilt at a cost of thirty-five million dollars. Furthermore, Quebec happened to be a more convenient place for President Roosevelt, as well as being more or less so for Prime Minister King. As for Prime Minister Churchill—he was everywhere and a trip to Quebec was but a detour for him.

At no time were the deliberations of the Three held in the Château Frontenac. The old chambers of the Citadel were witnesses to these meetings of destiny, and perhaps it was but right that these knights of the twentieth century should hide themselves in the stronghold of the land to make their plans to outwit the enemy.

One of the residences of the Lieutenant-Governor of the Province of Quebec which is located within the Citadel became the personal quarters of the great men. The Foreign Ministers and other delegates, the Chiefs of Staff of Army, Navy and Air Force were housed and held their meetings in the Château Frontenac. Important social functions were held there, such as Mr. Anthony Eden's dinner for Mr. Cordell Hull; the luncheon of the British Chiefs of Staff for the American Chiefs of Staff; the private dinner given by Premier King to Dr. T. V. Soong, China's Foreign Minister.

The names of the persons who, for more than two momentous weeks, thronged the Château Frontenac at that time, will go down in history, and it is only fitting, therefore, that they should be recorded in this history of the Castle of Quebec.

The delegation from the United States consisted of the Joint Chiefs of Staff:[3] Admirals W. D. Leahy and E. J. King; General G. C. Marshall, Army Chief of Staff; General H. H. Arnold, Army-

[3]Ranks and positions here given are those held at that time.

Air Forces Chief of Staff; the Committee of U.S.A. Service Forces: Lieutenant-General B. B. Somervell, Chief of Supply and Service Troops; Brigadier General W. A. Wood, Jr.; Colonel Marcus Stokes, Lieutenant-Colonel F. A. Bogart and Major E. M. Conklin; the Joint Staff Planners: Rear Admiral C. M. Cooke, Jr.; Brigadier-Generals A. C. Wedemeyer and L. S. Kuter; Colonel Adrian Williamson; Strategic Survey Committee: Vice-Admiral Russell Willson; Lieutenant-Commander J. J. Shaffer, Major-General M. S. Fairchild.

From Great Britain there came the Right Honourable Anthony Eden, Secretary of State for Foreign Affairs; Sir Alexander Cadogan, Under Secretary of State for Foreign Affairs; the Right Honourable Lord Leathers, Minister of War Transport; the Chiefs of Staff: General Sir Alan Brooke, chief of Imperial General Staff; Admiral of the Fleet Sir Dudley Pound, First Lord of the Admiralty and Chief of Naval Staff; Air Marshal Sir Charles Portal, Chief of Air Staff; Vice-Admiral Lord Louis Mountbatten, Chief of Combined Operations; Lieutenant-General Sir Hastings Ismay, Chief of Staff to the Minister of Defence; Field-Marshal Sir John Dill, Washington representative of Chiefs of Staff, head of the Joint Mission.

Canada was represented by Colonel the Honourable J. L. Ralston, Minister of National Defence; Major the Honourable C. G. Power, Minister of National Defence for Air; the Honourable C. D. Howe, Minister of Munitions and Supply; the Honourable T. A. Crerar, Minister of Mines and Resources; the Honourable J. L. Ilsley, Minister of Finance; the Honourable J. E. Michaud, Minister of Transport; the Honourable L. S. St. Laurent, Minister of Justice; Mr. N. A. Robertson, Under-Secretary of State for External Affairs; Dr. E. H. Coleman, Under-Secretary of State for Canada; Chiefs of Staff: Vice-Admiral P. W. Nelles, Chief of Naval Staff; Lieutenant-General K. Stuart, Chief of General Staff; Air Marshal L. S. Breadner, Chief of Air Staff.

Of great importance to the affairs of the Conference, each in his own sphere, were such personages as the Right Honourable Brendan Bracken, British Minister of Information; the Honourable Ray Atherton, United States Minister to Canada; Rear Admiral

Willson-Brown; the Honourable Leighton McCarthy; Mr. Harry Hopkins, Presidential Advisor; Mr. Stephen Early; General Laverick of Australia; Dr. T. V. Soong, China's Foreign Minister; Wing Commander Guy Gibson, V.C.; Sir John Anderson, Lord President of the British Council, and Member of the War Cabinet; Mr. Cordell Hull, United States Secretary of Foreign Affairs; Mr. H. L. Stimson, United States Secretary of War; Sir William Glasgow, Australian High Commissioner to Canada; Colonel Frank Knox, Secretary of United States Navy.

On August 10th, Prime Minister Churchill, Mrs. Churchill and their daughter, Subaltern Mary Churchill, ATS, arrived in Mr. Churchill's favourite Red Train, and were taken to the Lieutenant-Governor's Residence in the Citadel where they were welcomed by Prime Minister King. At the same time, members of the British Delegation were being welcomed to the Château Frontenac by the Canadian delegation.

President Roosevelt did not arrive until August 17th. Prior to his arrival he had been visited by Prime Minister Churchill at his home in Hyde Park where pre-Conference talks were held.

For two days, August 14th to 16th, the rumour made the rounds that the elusive Mr. Stalin was on his way to the Conference, but a news report from Moscow abruptly refuted it. There is no doubt that he had been invited—but the world had yet to learn that Mr. Stalin does not say "Yes" so easily.

Mr. Stalin did not come—but Falla did! And Falla was the most charming of Scotch terriers. A special Ambassador of Good Will, he made friends and romped and posed for photographers when all around him was seriousness and concentration, when those who absently patted his head were thinking things more deadly than ever dog or Nazi dreamed.

By the following year, 1944, the prosecution of the war against the enemy had reached such a status that the leaders of the nations must devise a climax—and soon—and devise it well lest they be outwitted and the battle go against them even when victory was in sight.

Mindful of the convenience, the quietness, the seclusion of Quebec, and the successes which had followed the plans made at their meeting there in 1943, the men of history once more turned their eyes to Canada, once more planned a rendezvous. Thirteen months from the date of the first meeting, Mr. Roosevelt, Mr. Churchill, Mr. King, and their staffs, together with the Chiefs of Staff for Army, Navy and Air Force, were again in Conference in the Citadel and Castle of Quebec. The eyes of the world turned again to the old city—anticipating—hoping that it forecast . . . *victory*.

It was a much briefer meeting this time. The Château was commandeered by the Canadian Government for only ten days, and the same arrangements were more easily put into effect owing to the experience of the previous meeting. Mrs. Eleanor Roosevelt came this time, and she and Mrs. Churchill each made a radio address and attended most of the few functions held in the Château.

Security precautions about the Château and Citadel were as rigorous, and the two focal points where the deliberators met and resided were as heavily guarded as before.

The final result of this conference was the longed-for conclusion two years later of World War II.

****

On a bleak day in January, 1947,[4] in the second year of a querulous peace, another plaque found a place of honour on the stone wall of the Château Frontenac on the courtyard side—a spot not far from the ancient Maltese Cross. The inscription is in two sections, in English and French, divided by a single flaming torch:

Headquarters of
Staffs of Armed
Forces present at
Quebec Conferences
August 1943 and
September 1944 to
Advise on Strategy
Vital to Victory
Franklin D. Roosevelt, President
of the United States and
Winston S. Churchill, Prime Minister
of Great Britain, Guests of
the Canadian Government.
W. L. Mackenzie King, Prime Minister.

Quartiers Généraux
des Etats-Majors
Des Forces Armées
Qui Prirent Part aux
Conférences de Québec
en Août 1943 et
Septembre 1944 pour y
Discuter les Questions
de Stratégie essen-
tielles à la Victoire
Franklin D. Roosevelt, Président des
Etats-Unis, et Winston S. Churchill,
Premier Ministre de Grande-Bretagne,
Hôtes du Canada à la Citadelle, Les
invités du Gouvernement Canadien.
W. L. Mackenzie King, Premier Ministre.

****

[4]January 18, 1947.

It is a fabulous place, this City of Quebec. It is steeped in history, rich in lore and legend. It offers a wide blue river sweeping down between twin heights; an old, old city that scrambles up the height, defying the laws of gravitation; an ancient fortress with high stone walls and a network of underground tunnels wending for miles under the city; habitant homes; wayside shrines. . . . And there is the Château Frontenac, the Castle of Quebec, standing on soil hallowed by the memory of Champlain, Montmagny, Frontenac, Haldimand, Van Horne, Shaughnessy . . . a hostelry where modern and mediaeval are inseparable . . . where past and present go forward together.

Above me looms the fortress, scarp and walls,
Dim, undefined in gloom of murky light.
No blare of gun or trumpet wakes the night,
In vain I hark to catch the sentry calls.
No camp fires glow at Montmorenci Falls,
No foe lurks now on yonder Levis height.
The city sleeps at peace, no war's affright
Shadows its dreams or timid heart appals.
Yet here in monument of bronze and stone,
The sieges fierce, the many battles fought,
Heroic deeds, and hero's names, record.
The victor and the vanquished we enthrone.
Time's cycle has its subtle changes wrought!
Two races dwell together in accord.[5]

****

[5]Poem from *Gleanings from Quebec* by G. M. Fairchild's (1908)

ACKNOWLEDGMENTS

THE AUTHOR is deeply indebted to all who have assisted in the preparation of *Castle of Quebec.*

Mr. G. J. Jessop, present Manager of the Château Frontenac Hotel in Quebec City, whose idea it was that the story of the Château Frontenac should be written, showed me consideration in all matters for which I am most grateful.

My warmest thanks go to Mr. E. C. Woodley, historian, Montreal, for his kindly advice, patience and encouragement; to Mr. Pierre-Georges Roy, historian, Levis, whose informative letters were most helpful; to Mr. Antoine Roy, Archivist of the Province of Quebec; Mr. J. A. Pelletier of the Provincial Museum, Quebec City; Mr. Norman Fee, Mr. Pierre Brunet and Mr. H. W. Gregory of the Public Archives of Canada, Ottawa, for information, maps, prints, etc.

Without the assistance of the Canadian Pacific Railway Company this book could not have been written. Of this Company, Mr. R. A. Mackie, Mr. L. G. Prevost, K.C., Mr. A. M. Irwin, Mr. J. A. Lafrenière and Mr. Harry Joyce, are especially deserving of my sincerest thanks for material and for their personal interest in the work.

My gratitude also goes to Lord Dorchester, descendant of Sir Guy Carleton, for much information and advice given during a personal interview; to Mr. Gordon Reed, Montreal, for information on the life of his mother, Mrs. Hayter Reed; to Mr. Pierre Dionne, Quebec City, for lending me the works of his father, Dr. N. E. Dionne; to Dr. G. A. Ramsay, London, Ontario, for material and encouragement.

To the Honourable Mr. Justice G. F. Gibsone, and Miss Evelyn Strachan, of the Literary and Historical Society of Quebec, for their help and consideration; to Mr. J. Paul Drouin, Montreal, for help in translations; and to Miss Vera Porritt, B.A., Montreal, for help in proof-reading, my warmest thanks.

Finally, to all the faithful historians of the past whose works have unfolded for me the Quebec of yesteryear, my humblest appreciation.

J. E. M.

Quebec City, P.Q.

INDEX

BIBLIOGRAPHY

Bender, L. P. *Old and New Canada, 1753-1844*. Montreal: Dawson Bros. 1882.
Bouchette, J. *Topography of Quebec*. London: W. Faden, 1815.
Bradley, A. G. *Lord Dorchester: Makers of Canada, Vol. V*. Toronto: Morang & Co., 1907.
Brooke, Frances. *History of Emily Montague*. Ottawa: Graphic Publishers Ltd., 1931.
Charlevoix, P. F. X. de *History and General Description of New France,* trans. by Dr. J. G. Shea. New York: Harper, 1900.
Christie, R. *History of the Late Province of Lower Canada, Vols. I-V,* Quebec: John Lovell, 1854
Cockburn, A. P. *Political Annals of Canada*. Toronto: Wm. Briggs, 1905.
De Celles, A. *'Patriotes' of '37*. Toronto: Glasgow, Brook & Co., 1922.
Dionne, N. E. *Samuel de Champlain: Makers of Canada, Vol. I*. Toronto: Morang & Co., 1911.

Doughty, A. G. *Cradle of New France.* Montreal: Cambridge Corp. Ltd., 1908; *Historical Journal of the Campaigns in North America by Captain John Knox, 2 vols.* Toronto: Champlain Society, 1914; *Quebec of Yester-Year.* Toronto: Thos. Nelson & Sons, Ltd., 1932.

Doughty, A. G. and Dionne, N. E., *Quebec Under Two Flags.* Quebec: Quebec News Co., 1903.

Douglas, James. *New England and New France.* New York and London: G. P. Putnam Sons, 1913; *Old France in the New World.* Cleveland and London: Burrows Bros. Co., 1905.

Ferland, J. B. A. *Cours d'Histoire du Canada.* Quebec: A. Coté, 1861.

Gagnon, Ernest. *Fort et Château St. Louis.* Montreal: Beauchemin, 1908.

Gale, George. *Historic Tales of Old Quebec, 1920; Quebec 'Twixt Old and New, 1915.* Quebec: Telegraph Printing Co.

Garneau, F. X. *Histoire du Canada.* Montreal: Beauchemin, 1882.

Grant, G. M. *Picturesque Canada.* Toronto: Belden Bros., 1882.

Hawkins, A. *Hawkins' Picture of Quebec, with Historical Recollections.* Quebec: Neilson & Cowan, 1834.

Kalm, P. *Travels into North America.* New York: Wilson-Erickson, 1937.

Kingsford, Wm. *History of Canada, 10 vols.* Toronto: Rowsell & Hutchison, 1887-1898

Lambert, John. *Travels Through Lower Canada and the United States of North America in the Years 1806, 1807, 1808.* London: T. Gillett, 1810.

Laverdiere, l'Abbe C. H. *Oeuvres de Champlain.* Quebec: G. E. Desbarats, 1870.

Le Moine, J. M. *The Explorations.* Quebec: Demers, 1889; *Maple Leaves.* Quebec: F. Carrel, 1863-1906; *Picturesque Quebec.* Montreal: Dawson Bros., 1882; *The Port of Quebec, Its Annals, 1535-1900.* Quebec: Chronicle Printing Co., 1901; *Quebec Past and Present.* Quebec: A. Coté & Co., 1876.

Leggo, Wm. *History of the Administration of the Earl of Dufferin.* Toronto: Lovell Printing and Pub. Co., 1878.

Lucas, Sir C. P. *Lord Durham's Report, 3 vols.* Oxford: Clarendon Press, 1912.

McIlwraith, J. N. *Sir Frederick Haldimand.* Toronto: Morang & Co., 1904.

Myrand, E. *Frontenac et Ses Amis.* Quebec: Dussault & Proulx, 1902.

Parker, Gilbert and Bryan, C. G. *Old Quebec, the Fortress of New France.* London: Macmillan & Co., 1903.

Parkman, Francis. *Count Frontenac and New France Under Louis XIV,* 1887; *Montcalm and Wolfe,* 1894; *The Old Régime in Canada,* 1892; *Pioneers of France in the New World, 1892.* Boston: Little, Brown & Co.

Roberts, C. G. D. *History of Canada.* Boston, New York, London: Lamson, Wolffe and Co., 1897.

Robertson, J. Ross. *History of the Knights Templars of Canada.* Toronto: Hunter, Rose & Co., 1890.

Roy, P. G. *Le Vieux Québec.* Quebec: Le Service des Archives, 1923.

Shortt, Adam. *Lord Sydenham: Makers of Canada, Vol. XV.* Toronto: Morang & Co., 1908.

Smith, Wm. *History of Canada.* Quebec: John Neilson, 1815.

Sulte, B. *History of Quebec, Its Resources and People.* Montreal, Toronto: Canada History Co., 1908.

Tuttle, C. R. *Illustrated History of the Dominion.* Montreal: Downie & Co., 1877-79; Boston: Tuttle & Downie, 1887.

Wallace, W. S. *Dictionary of Canadian Biography.* Toronto: Macmillan Co. of Canada Ltd., 1945.

Weld, Isaac, Jr. *Travels Through the States of North America, and the Provinces of Upper and Lower Canada During the Years 1795, 1796 and 1797.* London: John Stockdale, 1799.

Withrow, W. H. *Popular History of the Dominion of Canada.* Toronto: Wm. Briggs, 1884.

Wood, Wm. *Storied Province of Quebec, 2 vols.* Toronto: Dominion Pub. Co. Ltd., 1931.

Woodley, E. C. *Province of Quebec Through Four Centuries.* Toronto: W. J. Gage & Co. Ltd., 1944.

Wrong, G. M. *Conquest of New France.* New Haven: Yale Univ. Press, 1918; *Rise and Fall of New France.* Toronto: Macmillan Co. of Canada Ltd., 1928.

25 8bre 1683
N° d'ordre 347
Echelle de 100 pieds
CARTE
DU FORT ST LOUIS
DE QUEBEC
Par Iean Baptiste Louis Franquelin
1683